Contents

Content guidance

Questions & Answers

Getting the most from this book

Examiner tips

Advice from the examiner on key points in the text to help you learn and recall unit content, avoid pitfalls, and polish your exam technique in order to boost your grade.

Knowledge check

Rapid-fire questions throughout the Content guidance section to check your understanding.

Knowledge check answers

1 Turn to the back of the book for the Knowledge check answers.

Summary

Summaries

● Each core topic is rounded off by a bullet-list summary for quick-check reference of what you need to know.

Questions & Answers

Exam-style questions

Examiner comments on the questions
Tips on what you need to do to gain full marks, indicated by the icon ⓔ.

Sample student answers
Practise the questions, then look at the student answers that follow each set of questions.

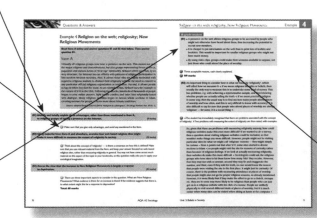

Examiner commentary on sample student answers
Find out how many marks each answer would be awarded in the exam and then read the examiner comments (preceded by the icon ⓔ) following each student answer. Annotations that link back to points made in the student answers show exactly how and where marks are gained or lost.

About this book

This unit guide is aimed at students taking the AQA A2 Sociology course. It covers the topic of **Beliefs in Society**, with a main focus on the sociology of religion, which is examined within Unit 3 (SCLY3). Beliefs in Society is one of the four choices of topic in the unit, the other three being Global Development, Mass Media, and Power and Politics. The topic is designed to give you a good understanding of the importance of religion, science and ideologies to individuals and to society as a whole, as well as the different types of religious organisations and beliefs and how these have changed over time.

How to use the guide

To benefit most from this guide, you need to use different parts of it at different stages of your course. From the beginning of your study of Beliefs in Society, you should look at the **Content guidance** section. This provides you with an overview of what is included in the specification for Beliefs in Society. It is designed to make you aware of what you should know before the unit examination. As you go through the topic, you should refer to the relevant part of the Content guidance section to check on your progress and to ensure that you have understood the main concepts used.

The **Question and Answer** section provides four sets of exam-type questions on Beliefs in Society for you to try, together with some sample answers at A-grade and C-grade level. Examiner's comments are included to show how marks are awarded at A2. To gain full advantage from this section, you should attempt to answer the questions progressively. Try to answer one or two sets of questions as you finish doing the topic of Beliefs in Society. This will help you to consolidate the knowledge you have gained and to organise your understanding of the topic in a systematic fashion. As you move into revision mode for the unit examination, attempt those questions that you have not done, as part of an active revision strategy.

To use the questions and answers effectively, you have to be honest and not look at the answers before you have attempted the question yourself. Study your chosen question carefully and then attempt to answer each part (or the whole question if it is an essay response) *without* looking first at the example answers provided. It is important that you work in this way — by comparing your answers with the specimen answers, you will understand what you might have done better and so improve your performance. When you have completed your answers, study the A-grade student's answers and identify where you might have made other links. Look carefully at the examiner's comments to see where you might have been able to make further improvements, giving particular thought to the different skills that you have to demonstrate. You should also look at the C-grade answers and, using the examiner's comments as a guide, rewrite them so that they would gain A-grade marks.

These activities are time-consuming and should not be rushed. It all means you divide up the tasks you have to do into manageable chunks and complete the activities over a number of weeks. Keep in mind that you will need to have everything completed in good time for the examination. You will therefore need to know on what date the

Unit 3 exam is to be held. You should then be able to fit these activities in with your other revision tasks.

In addition to using the questions to develop your examination skills, you could draw on the answers as a source of revision material. Reading through the A-grade student's answers should provide you with useful reminders of important sociological material. Remember, however, that in the exam you must answer the question that is on your paper — you should not try to reproduce the specimen answer.

The A2 specification

The aims of the A2 Sociology course are to enable you to:

- acquire knowledge and a critical understanding of contemporary social processes and social changes
- appreciate the significance of theoretical and conceptual issues in sociological debate
- understand and evaluate sociological methodology and a range of research methods through active involvement in the research process
- develop skills that enable individuals to focus on their personal identity, roles and responsibilities in society
- develop a lifelong interest in social issues

In addition, there should be an emphasis on contemporary society.

Content guidance

This section is intended to show you the major issues and themes covered in **Beliefs in Society** and the main points of evaluation that have been made about them. We have also identified the key concepts and key writers in each area. These are offered as guidance only. The points included are not exhaustive — you may raise other perfectly legitimate points. You will find many other concepts and studies that are relevant to your exploration of Beliefs in Society, including religion. The main studies and arguments in religion are well rehearsed in all the major textbooks, so you should have no trouble finding these out. Your teacher will also give you other studies during your course. The main magazine for A-level sociologists (*Sociology Review*) has repeatedly focused on the issues of religion, and so back copies, available from your school or college library, will be a useful source of information. It is always a good idea to read some original research on a particular topic and religion is full of interesting and accessible books and articles. If these are not available to you, most of the textbooks have good accounts of relevant ideas and arguments.

The content of the AQA A2 topic of Beliefs in Society falls into five main areas:

- theories of religion and belief
- the role of religion in societies and its relationship to social change and stability
- forms of religious organisation, including cults, sects, denominations, churches and New Age movements
- the relationship between social groups, religious beliefs and practices and religious/spiritual organisations
- the secularisation debate, in a global context

The topic is designed to give you a comprehensive understanding of the importance of these areas in contemporary and past societies. You are expected to be familiar with the major sociological explanations of religion and belief, in terms of their functions for society and for individuals. This will include the classical sociologists' views on religion, which they all thought was central to understanding the operation of societies, as well as more recent approaches such as postmodernism. There were strong differences of opinion among the classical sociologists as to whether religion brought people together or kept them apart, and whether it was a force for change or stability. You will also need to be familiar with the range of different religious organisations that exist and their relationship to various social groups. Last, one of the main debates in the sociology of religion is the continued importance of religion in contemporary societies and the contradictory evidence about the development of a secular society. This debate occurs at three levels — society, religious practices and individual consciousness.

Theories of religion

Definitions

Key ideas

Examiner tip
It is important that you are able to use concepts such as inclusivist and exclusivist correctly, so that your examination answers read like sociological responses to questions.

- Definitions are important because they decide what should be examined as a religious phenomenon and what should not.
- Inclusivist definitions include many phenomena that might seem controversial, such as magic, or even non-religious beliefs, such as communism.
- Exclusivist definitions exclude phenomena that do not make reference to a supernatural being and limit what can be defined as religious.
- Functional definitions of religion focus on the role that a religious phenomenon performs for society as a whole, such as acting as a unifying force.
- Substantive definitions refer to a defining characteristic, such as a belief in God, as the distinctive feature of religion.
- Inclusivist definitions are 'essentialist', that is, they take the position that religious belief and activity is a necessary feature of the human condition, although it may take many forms.
- Exclusivist definitions are 'non-essentialist', accepting that there may be a decline or growth in religious activity at different historical stages.
- Quasi-religions have a 'this world' orientation and can focus on sport, shopping, rock, television personalities etc.
- The definition adopted leads the sociologist to ask different questions about the scale and importance of religious belief and activity in society, and possibly to reach different conclusions.
- Religions can be seen as a form of ideology, serving the interests of a particular social group.

Knowledge check 1
Give an example of a 'quasi-religion'.

Ideology Systems of ideas that have the effect of encouraging actions that support the position of specific social groups.

Evaluation

- + Inclusivist-functionalist definitions allow the sociologist to investigate a wide range of historical and contemporary practices as 'religious', including humanism and psychoanalysis, because these are concerned with the 'ultimate problems' that confront all human beings.
- + Exclusivist-substantive definitions allow the sociologist to examine only those social phenomena that are commonsensically recognised as expressions of religious feeling.
- + Both approaches are attempting to identify what can be 'religious' in order to form a field of study with definite boundaries.
- − Inclusivist-functional definitions are drawn so wide that they make the idea of a specifically religious sphere of activity difficult to maintain — everything can be seen as 'religious'.

– Exclusivist-substantive definitions limit what can be seen as religious and lead inevitably to the idea that religious observance has declined in importance, as its manifestation changes in society.
– Both approaches are actually linked to ideological positions that are associated with either supporting or undermining religious belief.

Key concepts

inclusivism, exclusivism, functionalism, essentialism, transcendence

Key thinkers

Durkheim, Weber, Bellah, Yinger, Robertson, Hunt

Durkheim

Key ideas

- Durkheim started from the position that social existence was only possible through the belief in shared ideas.
- He offered a functionalist definition of religion, as being 'beliefs and practices which unite into one single moral community called a Church'.
- Religion was therefore an essential part of the 'conscience collective', or the shared ideas that make social life possible.
- These shared ideas constituted the fundamental notions of time, space, causation and relationships that allow humankind to think logically.
- He distinguished between the 'profane' and the 'sacred', the former being everyday life and the latter constituting things set apart and forbidden.
- He drew these ideas from a study of the totemic religions of the Australian aborigines, in which the totem worshipped was a representation of the clan.
- The totem also symbolised society and the **collective rituals** of religion. In this sense it was a restatement of the importance of social bonds.
- Religion therefore acted to bind individuals to society, allowing them to understand and enact correct social relations between individuals, through the shared values of religious belief.
- Religion also regulated behaviour so that social life became possible without selfish individualism getting in the way.

Evaluation

+ Durkheim offered a functional explanation in which religion is given a dominant role in social cohesion.
+ He identified a moral dimension to the nature of social relationships, based on religious ideas.

Examiner tip
Always define any concepts that are in the exam question as clearly and concisely as possible.

Knowledge check 2
Give an example of a sacred object.

Collective rituals
The formal activities that groups take part in to express their common understandings and reinforce their feelings of solidarity. The coronation of a king or queen is a collective ritual that embodies nationhood.

+ He explained the existence of religion in terms of its rituals rather than its theological ideas.
- Durkheim ignored the importance of individual religious experience.
- He had a static view of religion; for example, he did not attempt to explain the rise of new religions or religious leaders.
- The practices of primitive religions do not explain the workings of religion in a complex, religiously diverse modern society.

Key concepts

conscience collective, sacred, profane, totems, representation

Key thinkers

Durkheim, Eister

Weber and Weberian approaches

Key ideas

Knowledge check 3

What is meant by a 'system of production'?

- Weber believed that ideas, including religious ideas, had an independent effect on social and economic change.
- To demonstrate this, he examined the relationship between new religious ideas and the development of the capitalist system of production.
- Specifically he argued that the ethical orientation of Calvinist Protestants led to practices that gave impetus to capitalist modes of production — the 'spirit of capitalism'.
- Catholic culture was portrayed as being concerned with conspicuous consumption, whereas Protestantism encouraged a frugal frame of mind in which income was ploughed back into production rather than spent on luxuries.
- There was thus an 'elective affinity' between the Protestant ethic and the spirit of capitalism; the Protestant ethic was not the sole causal relationship, but an important factor.
- The ideas of Calvinism produced a particular personality trait that acted out patterns of conduct conducive to the development of capitalism.
- Weber also examined other religions to see if there were reasons why they did not lead to the development of capitalist modes of behaviour.
- Confucianism stressed adjustment to the world. By contrast, the uncertainty of Calvinism had the unintended consequence of leading believers to see worldly success as a sign of God's favour.
- Bellah argued that the relationship between religion and economics is indirect, operating through the political structure, rather than direct.
- Wertheim argued that all ideas, for example scientific thought, have a transformative capacity, not just religious ones.

Transformative capacity The potential of ideas or events to create fundamental changes in social arrangements.

Evaluation

+ Weber stressed the importance of ideas as causal factors in social developments, rejecting economic determinism.
+ He sought to explain social change as a complex interplay of forces, but in which there are decisive points in history that can be identified through sociological analysis.
+ Weber's argument offers a cross-cultural approach to social change, using data from a number of societies to explore a particular hypothesis and come to a conclusion.
− Weber did not demonstrate how strongly individual entrepreneurs held their religious beliefs and therefore whether these affected their patterns of behaviour.
− It has been claimed that the connection between religion and economics has been over-stressed, with many other factors suggested as the cause of capitalism.
− It has been argued that it was not the religious belief of the Calvinists that was important for the development of capitalism but their marginal position in a Catholic society that led them to strive for wealth.

Examiner tip
Make sure that your evaluations are fairly balanced when considering strengths and weaknesses.

Key concepts

Calvinistic Protestantism, spirit of capitalism, elective affinity, transformative capacity, cross-culturalism

Key thinkers

Weber, Tawney, Wertheim, Sombart

Marx

Key ideas

- Marx saw religion as an aspect of ideology, rather than as important in its own right.
- It was an important element in the 'false consciousness' of the workers and of the bourgeoisie, in that neither had a real appreciation of their position as pawns of the system.
- For the workers, religion was one way in which their alienation was alleviated, focusing their attention on the rewards of the next world rather than the misery of this one.
- However, religion also represented the workers' yearning for a better world, their hopes for a future better than their present situation.
- For the bourgeoisie, religion was a cloak of respectability behind which they relentlessly pursued profit at the expense of the workers.
- Protestantism, with its emphasis on the 'abstract individual' facing his or her maker alone, allowed the bourgeoisie to treat their workers not as men or women but as commodities to be bought and sold.

Knowledge check 4
Define alienation.

Bourgeoisie The social class that owns the means of production, such as factories and banks.

Examiner tip
When writing about
a particular approach,
including relevant, more
sophisticated elements will
improve your grade.

- Both bourgeoisie and proletariat were subject to the impersonal forces of capitalism, which destroyed and favoured individuals in an apparently random fashion for which no religion could compensate.
- Kautsky argued that it was the development of capitalism that led to the creation of Protestant ideas, to justify the economic activities of the bourgeoisie.

Evaluation

+ The phenomenon of religion is seen by Marxism as being determined by the economic base, so giving primary importance to economic activity rather than ideas.
+ The positions of both proletariat and bourgeoisie are explained in terms of the role of religion in an inhumane system.
+ Religion is a delusion of the mind, designed to resign individuals to their lot.
− Marxism dismisses the reality of sincere religious feelings that individuals experience.
− It is monocausal, explaining religion purely as an epiphenomenon of the economic system.
− Religion has an impact on social groups other than just social classes, such as ethnic groups, but these are not addressed.

Key concepts

alienation, bourgeoisie, proletariat, false consciousness

Key thinkers

Marx, Feuerbach, Kautsky

Functionalism

Key ideas

- Though drawn from Durkheim, functionalist thought on religion differs from Durkheim's views in certain crucial respects.
- Totemism is not a set of unified practices, as envisaged by Durkheim, but ranges from very complex formulations to trivial phenomena like totem poles.
- Totemism can also be seen not as the relation of the individual to the social world, but as expressing the individual's relationship to the natural world (Levi-Strauss).
- An alternative functionalist theory was put forward by Malinowski, who saw religion as the response of individuals to the uncertainty of the world, fulfilling an emotional need for security.
- Religion can function to bind individuals together in the face of the death of one member of a group, through the comfort of collective rituals.
- Religion therefore makes a unique contribution to social integration.

Knowledge check 5
Outline **two** aspects of
functionalist thought.

Social integration This
occurs when individuals
are bound together in
a society as a unified
whole, identifying with the
collective expressions of
society.

- Any decline in religious belief or practice leads to increased social disorganisation.
- Religion, therefore, is an essential feature of all successful societies.
- It is the only aspect of human experience that can grasp the non-empirical, and as such is a necessary basis for human action.

Evaluation

+ Functionalism insists on looking at the social dimension rather than the individual for an explanation of religion.
+ By emphasising the importance of religion in social integration, it answers the Hobbesian 'problem of order' of how we can live together peacefully.
+ It deals with the supernatural as a 'real' phenomenon of subjective experience.
- Many societies seem to exist without a unifying religion in the conventional sense.
- Functionalism asserts rather than explains how religion reinforces common values, especially in multireligious societies.
- Religious participation can exist without any corresponding strong religious belief.

Key concepts

totemism, social integration, the supernatural, social disorganisation

Key thinkers

Durkheim, Radcliffe-Brown, Levi-Strauss, Malinowski, Davis, Parsons, Bellah

Interactionism

Key Ideas

Phenomenologists focus on the states of consciousness of individuals, including their religious consciousness, as they live out their everyday lives in the Lebenswelt.

- Religion is established by human enterprise or actions, in which objects or beings are given awesome power, standing apart from, but related to, the existence of humanity.
- This sacred dimension is the opposite of the chaos that confronts individuals as they try to make sense of their lives.
- Religion therefore gives us ultimate meanings, making the universe manageable by reducing it to a human-centred enterprise, in which we gain significance in the cosmic order.
- A higher plane of existence is indicated by many aspects of human experience — when we discover order in our lives, from the joy of play, from hope, from events experienced as evil, from humour.
- Religion is therefore about cognition, providing us all with the categories and concepts needed to make sense of the world.

Examiner tip
Organise your revision by establishing a timetable for the 2 months before the examination — plan for all your subjects and also some free time for yourself.

Lebenswelt The 'life-world', the mass of dense interactions between people that make up everyday life and which individuals take for granted.

Knowledge check 6

What do you understand by the term 'existential'?

Examiner tip

Develop a consistent way of taking notes. A good set of notes is the basis of success in the examination.

- We all share these existential concerns (what is life, death, joy, suffering etc.) and all therefore have religiosity — a sense of the supernatural.
- As an individual phenomenon, contemporary religion has many of the features of a supermarket, in which individuals are free to choose or change according to personal inclination.

Evaluation

+ Interactionists take religious feeling and sensibility as a 'real' phenomenon experienced by people, rather than as a false consciousness.
+ Interactionism deals with the issue of 'ultimate meaning' rather than taking a strictly materialist approach.
+ It takes religion as an everyday activity rather than at the level of the institution.
− Interactionists place too much emphasis on the subjective meaning of religion, ignoring its power and influence on the institutional level, for example.
− Phenomenological approaches suffer from 'cognitive reductionism', over-emphasising the rational/thoughtful aspects of religion, against its emotional appeal.
− Interactionism assumes that we all have a measure of religious feeling that must be fulfilled, when, in fact, religious sensibility can be shown to be distributed according to social class.

Key concepts

Lebenswelt, everyday world, spiritual supermarket, cognitive reductionism

Key thinkers

Berger, Berger and Luckmann, Turner, Bibby, Beckford

Postmodernism

Key ideas

- With the collapse of religious certainty represented by the 'sacred canopy' of a universally accepted religion, individuals have to seek their own 'meaning-routes' through the wealth of religious choices on offer.
- As the old religious certainties fade, new forms of religious connectedness are made between individuals, either referring back to certainty or rejecting it in favour of the individual quest for truth.
- In a **network society**, where flows of power, wealth and information are beyond individual control, individuals may turn to the power of religious identity to try to exercise some control over their situation.
- As religion becomes 'à la carte', the choice is between forms of haute cuisine (traditional religion) and McDonaldisation (standardised but bland religious ideas).

Network society
A society composed of interactions rather than structures, in which power is not a feature of the hierarchical structure of society but is shown in the actions between groups and individuals.

- In a postmodern world of endless choice, religious fundamentalism is not a 'throwback' but a rational response to 'choice overload', where the individual has to make myriad choices not only of consumer products, but also between ideas and values.
- The media are a crucial aspect of postmodern religion, with some sociologists seeing the internet as a new metaphor for the nature of God, being decentralised and dispersed (Turkle).
- As religion becomes packaged as a commodity in the market place, it becomes Disneyfied, that is, trivial and crowd-pleasing.
- Globalisation trends are reflected in the emergence of new religious movements that look for a unifying and common religious culture under such names as Gaia or planetary theology.

Knowledge check 7

Identify **two** aspects of what sociologists refer to as globalisation.

Evaluation

+ Postmodernism seeks to explain the explosion of religious sects and cults in contemporary capitalist societies.
+ It locates movements such as fundamentalism and planetary ecology within the conditions of contemporary postmodern living.
+ It emphasises the importance of the hyper-reality of the media in contemporary religious life.
- It overemphasises the degree to which the old certainties have collapsed and we are faced with genuine choices.
- Fundamentalism can be seen as a reactionary response to modernism, rather than a postmodern response to choice.
- Postmodernism denies the serious way in which individuals approach religion in favour of a 'playful' perspective.

Examiner tip

Before you start preparing for the exam, make sure that you are aware of what the awarding body — AQA — specifies for the examination. Get yourself a copy of the specification, which is downloadable from the internet.

Key concepts

network society, 'à la carte' religion, choice overload, McDonaldisation, Disneyfication

Key thinkers

Bauman, Castells, Limieux, Heelas, Turkle, Lyon

- Definitions of religion are important because they influence what questions are likely to be asked about the role of religion in modern society.
- The sociology of religion was of interest to classical sociologists, although they took very different positions about it.
- The main divisions are between those who see religion as a force for stability and those who see it as a force for change.

- The study of religion occurs both at the level of society and at the level of the individual.
- Religions have traditionally been organised around geographical areas, but in a postmodern world, religions are now dispersed throughout the world and have diversified into many different forms.

Summary

The role of religion

As a unifying force

Key ideas

- Where there is a 'sacred canopy' of a universal religion in a society, it can act as a force for solidarity.
- A common religion offers a set of values that shapes behaviour in a specific way, so that all are agreed on appropriate conduct.
- This can lead to a form of mechanistic solidarity in society, in which there is an identification through sameness, based on religious belief.
- Secular formations, such as the monarchy, use religious symbolism to reinforce their claim to represent the nation and act as a focus of loyalty.
- In a global society of mass migrations, religion can act as a unifying force for disparate populations; for example when an allegiance to Islam assists marginal populations to carve out an identity.
- The importance of Christianity in the USA is that it acts as a unifier of a mainly immigrant society, despite differences in the particular form of Christianity adopted.
- **Diasporic** populations, such as the Jews, use religion as a marker for identity, despite surface differences between forms of the religion, such as Orthodox or liberal or reform Judaism.
- In divided societies, such as Ireland, religion can act as a signifier, uniting distinct populations in opposition to the 'Other'.
- Secular ideologies have sought to replace religion as a unifying force. Communism, for example, took on many aspects of religion, such as the 'saints' of Marx, Engels and Lenin.

Evaluation

+ This view emphasises the positive aspects of religion, showing it as a force for integration, identity and solidarity.
+ It explains the persistence of religious differences in populations characterised by migration.
+ It focuses on the common elements that members of a religion share, through an acceptance of shared ideas and allegiances.
− The idea of a unifying religious force is more appropriate for historical societies than for contemporary ones.
− The 'sacred canopy' idea overestimates the degree of real loyalty to and belief in an overarching religion, such as Catholicism in medieval Europe, as individuals often only pay lip-service to such beliefs.
− The history of religion suggests that it is more significant for its ability to divide people than unite them, as in religious wars or the contemporary Middle East.

Knowledge check 8

What is meant by organic solidarity?

Diasporic Scattered or geographically dispersed populations, e.g. Jews, Armenians, Kurds.

Examiner tip

Read some sociology every week, focusing on what particularly interests you about a topic. This will help you to express yourself sociologically in the exam.

Key concepts

integration, sacred canopy, diaspora, global society

Key thinkers

Durkheim, Shils, Parsons, Bellah

As a source of conflict

Key ideas

- Strong faith in a particular religion often involves a deep belief in the 'wrongness' of other religious forms, expressed in such terms as heresy, abomination and false belief.
- Religion can generate strong collective feelings that function to separate out often minority groups from mainstream society, so that conflict occurs over the allocation of resources to particular religious segments of the community.
- Religious allegiance often parallels other social divisions, particularly of class and ethnicity, compounding the potential for misunderstanding and conflict.
- Many religious faiths have a powerful 'missionary' zeal associated with them, in which adherents are called upon to proselytise (convert) the non-believer, by force if necessary.
- Historically and in contemporary politics, many wars have been and are fought in the name of religion; for example, the conflict in the Middle East and the 'war against terrorism' have a religious dimension to them.
- Where religions have an eschatological dimension (a belief in the end of the world), believers may be careless of their own earthly lives and strive for immortality through violent actions against those they identify as the religious enemy.
- Marxists claim that religious conflicts mask economic conflicts and therefore act as a smokescreen for the exploitation of the have-nots by the haves.
- Where there is a strong 'state' religion, in which one form of religious belief is given privileges by the state over all others, members of other religions may suffer discrimination or disadvantage; for example, in Great Britain a Roman Catholic cannot legally become the monarch.
- Religion is often mixed up with cultural struggles over what is correct behaviour and beliefs for individuals, as evidenced in the fatwa against Salman Rushdie.
- Many contemporary believers feel threatened by secular forces undermining their core beliefs, such as the 'culture war' in the USA over gay marriage.

Evaluation

- + This view focuses on the history of religions rather than the idealism of their theology or ideology.
- + It suggests that religions have a 'dark side' and are not all peace and love to humankind.

Knowledge check 9

What is the religious organisation that has a formal place in the government of Britain?

Economic conflict This occurs over the allocation of resources in society between different groups and individuals and may take place over money, goods, housing, access to education, ownership of production etc.

Examiner tip

Review your notes at regular intervals. This will help you to learn the material you need for the examination.

+ It directs attention to the consequences of religious discrimination and the disadvantages that members of particular faiths may experience in society.
– It downplays the real good that religions have achieved in the world, in terms of both religious organisations and individual believers.
– It assumes that adherents to different religions are inevitably drawn into conflict through their religious differences.
– It ignores movements, such as ecumenicalism, that seek to forge bridges not just within different sections of the same world religions, but between members of all faiths.

Key concepts

fundamentalism, religion as a smokescreen, exclusivist religion

Key thinkers

Marx, Kepel, Wallis, Bromley and Shupe

As a conservative force

Key ideas

- The notion of religion as a conservative force is based on the links in many societies between the state and a specific religion, where there are pervasive political, social and economic connections between high-ranking members of the religion and political personalities.
- It is related to functionalist ideas that religion serves to integrate individuals into a dominant status quo, but goes further in arguing that religion seeks to defend political and social arrangements as they are.
- Religion thus has an important legitimising function for many regimes. For example, some claim that Methodism, because of its conservative nature, was the main reason why the working classes did not revolt in nineteenth-century Britain.
- The classic example of the fusion of religious and political power is in the Vatican State, where the Papacy is both a temporal and a spiritual phenomenon.
- The involvement of Evangelical Christians in right-wing politics in the USA is seen as one of the main manifestations of contemporary religious conservatism.
- This identification of religion with the status quo has led in some instances to the dominant religion of a society being associated with authoritarian and occasionally violent political regimes, such as in the case of Pinochet's Chile.
- The Iranian revolution of Ayatollah Khomenei can be seen either as a conservative revolution in defence of traditional Islamic values or as a reactionary movement against the modernisation and Westernisation of Iran by the Shah.
- There is also a wider sense in which religion can be seen as a conservative force, in that many long-established religions act in defence of 'traditional' values and ways of behaving and are often critical of modernising tendencies, such as Taliban rule in Afghanistan.

Knowledge check 10
What do sociologists mean by 'legitimising'?

Traditional values In the sociology of religion these often refer to those beliefs that are contained within the holy book of a religion, as interpreted through its history.

- The traditional conservative values of many religions seem to conflict with modern and postmodern ways of living, but are also powerful attractions to many individuals who are bemused by the lack of certainty in their lives.
- Many individuals are able to adhere to the conservative message of their religious beliefs while acting in ways that are contrary to them. Many Roman Catholics, for example, practise birth control, which is barred by the Catholic Church.
- Secular ideologies can also act as a conservative force, even when apparently 'revolutionary', once their adherents have taken power; for example, the USSR before the downfall of communism.

Examiner tip

Produce reduced versions of your notes. These will help you to revise later on.

Evaluation

+ This view places an emphasis on tradition and continuity that has a wide appeal in conditions of change.
+ It locates allegiance to a particular state in a religious context, thus legitimising and securing it against discontent and rebellion.
+ It identifies values that seem to have endured for many years and act as a call to 'correct behaviour'.
- The conservative leanings of many religious personalities have led to their defence of some unpleasant regimes that have little respect for human rights.
- Unquestioning support for the way things have always been impedes progress in many spheres of social life, for example in women's rights.
- Values that are unchanging are likely to conflict with changing social conditions and lead to misery for individuals as they juggle their beliefs and their way of life.

Key concepts

universal church, religious reaction, legitimation, anti-modernity, Westernisation

Key thinkers

Parsons, Troeltsch, Yinger, Halevy

As a source of change

Key ideas

- Drawn from the work of Weber, this approach emphasises the role of religion in stimulating social, political or economic change through the evolution of new religious ideas.
- It is associated with the thesis of the 'spirit of capitalism', in which the emergence of Calvinism acted as a spur to the development of capitalist modes of behaviour that transformed feudal societies.
- This view of religions is based on the idea that they contain within them the potential for both reactionary and radical actions, and therefore religious believers can be mobilised for progressive causes.

Knowledge check 11

Give **two** examples of 'capitalist modes of behaviour'.

Apartheid A system
of racial segregation
and discrimination that
disenfranchised and
oppressed the black
majority of South Africa.

Examiner tip
Practise doing examination
questions on a regular
basis.

- Liberation theology of the 1960s and 1970s is seen as an example of the 'commitment to the poor' by worker-priests and nuns in Latin America, which led many grass-root leaders of the Roman Catholic church to involve themselves in radical and even revolutionary movements.
- With an emphasis on justice, many religious movements, such as the World Council of Churches, supported the anti-apartheid movement in South Africa.
- Where religion forms an oppositional focus to repressive regimes, it can be used for political change, even where it is violent, such as in the Iranian revolution.
- Religious organisations also formed the basis of many anti-colonial movements in Africa, such as Alice Lenshina's Church in Zambia, where the mix of Christian and traditional religious forms was tried to establish an authentic African voice.
- Religion also formed the core of resistance of native Americans to encroachment by white society during the 'Ghost Dances' in the late nineteenth century.
- Scientific ideas have been, and continue to be, a massive source of change in societies, for example the growth of the internet or the potential of stem cell research to change individual destiny.

Evaluation

+ This approach acknowledges the contradictory potential of religion for both conservative and radical ends.
+ It develops a historical perspective in understanding the nature of religion as a tool of the oppressed to resist their condition.
+ It offers a positive view of religion's role in society, stressing its potential for achieving essential changes needed to promote values, such as justice, which are both secular and religious.
− It tends to overestimate the success of religious movements in promoting social change, as in Latin America where liberation theology has been essentially neutralised.
− It sees social change as an end in its own right, without examining the consequences of such change for the people it is supposed to assist, for example justifying repressive regimes that might emerge as a result.
− It downplays other forces for social change in favour of religion, negating economic and political movements such as the anti-colonial movement.

Key concepts

mobilisation, commitment to the poor, liberation theology

Key thinkers

Weber, Wilson, Debray, Mooney

- Religions have often united people who live within a particular society and have acted as a focus of identity and solidarity.
- They have also been a source of disagreement and conflict, leading to outbreaks of war and cruelty in the name of religion.
- Religions can act as a brake on social change, emphasising what has 'always been' and being hostile to new social realities, such as the changing role of women.
- Religion can also foster change and create new social conditions when it expresses individuals' desire to make things better.

Religious organisations

Church and sect

Key ideas

- A fundamental distinction in Christian religious organisations is the difference between church and sect as elaborated by Troeltsch
- Both churches and sects believe that only their members will gain salvation and that the adherents of other organisations or religions will not be in a 'state of grace'.
- Churches believe that salvation is given in a mystical manner as an infant is received through baptism into the pre-existing church ('salvation through grace'). The individual is therefore born into the church, experiencing it as an objective reality with a long tradition.
- Sects believe that salvation depends upon the rational assent of the adult individual to believe in a personal God and to live in a voluntary community of 'saints', made up of the other believers ('salvation through faith').
- Churches are positive in their attitudes towards the established social order, often having formal links with the state. In some cases their higher personnel are drawn from the upper classes.
- Sects are more associated with lower social classes, separate from the establishment, and have a more tense relationship with the state, sometimes being in strong opposition to the secular order.
- Churches develop ideologies to defend and legitimate the status quo, such as the **divine right of kings** in monarchical societies. These ideologies may become outdated, but are retained as part of the tradition of the church.
- Sects tend not to look to the past but to live in the present, 'living the life' of faith, with their values constantly being renewed as a result of their everyday experiences of God's presence.
- Churches and sects should not be seen only in uniform terms, nor as resistant to change. Churches have within them enthusiastic and evangelical elements, while sects are subject to routinisation and also have a formal element.

> **Knowledge check 12**
>
> What do you understand by the term 'objective reality'?

> **Divine right of kings**
> The belief that the monarch had been appointed directly by God and therefore any resistance to his or her rule was not only treasonable, but also sinful.

Evaluation

+ This distinction identifies key respects in which religious organisations may differ.

+ It is a useful tool to use when beginning to analyse the behaviour and ideas of religious organisations.

+ It focuses on the social dimension of religious organisations, examining their relationship with social hierarchies.

− The distinction is more appropriate to an earlier period of history, when, during the Reformation, Europeans were divided between a Catholic church and oppositional Protestant sects.

− It does not take account of the dynamics of religious organisations, which can change their forms over time, with churches becoming more sect-like and vice versa.

− Sects are less persecuted in contemporary Western societies and may therefore have lost their antipathy to the state.

Key concepts

legitimation, opposition, salvation through grace, salvation through faith, routinisation

Key thinkers

Weber, Troeltsch, Barker

Denominations and cults

Key ideas

- Denominations were described by Niebuhr as 'a compromise between Christianity and the world' to indicate that they were distinctive from and somewhere between the formalism of churches and the inspirationalism of sects.

- Originally sect-like in their religious devotion, as the second generation was born they took on more of the attributes of churches.

Inspirationalism A form of religious worship that emphasises a personal relationship with God that manifests itself sometimes in high energy outpourings of joy, speaking in tongues etc.

- The crucial issue that turned some sects towards more routinised forms of worship was that of baptising infants. While sects emphasised adult baptism, some members wanted their children to be brought up in the organisation and used infant baptism as a sign of their commitment. This turned them to more church-like practices, which came to be associated with denominations.

- The growing wealth of sect members, as they lived frugal and productive lives in their faith, eventually contributed to the development of many sects into more formal denominations.

- However, there was no inevitability in this process. Wealthy sects could retain their sect-like character or renew their enthusiasm rather than become routinised.

- Denominations are distinct from sects and churches in their non-universalist approach; that is, they accept that there are other ways to salvation than just through membership of their specific organisation.

- A further complication of any typology is the existence of cults.
- Cults were originally a private form of religion, usually with a mystic dimension.
- 'Cult' is widely used now to indicate secretive and domineering sect-like organisations that may operate with manipulative mind-control techniques and have a highly exclusivist agenda, cutting off adherents from family non-believers.
- Wallis classifics churches, sects, denominations and cults according to whether the wider world sees them as being respectable (church and denomination) or deviant (sects and cults), as well as whether they see themselves as being the only road to salvation (church and sect) or not (denomination and cult).

Evaluation

+ These categories add to our understanding of the complexity of types of religious organisation.
+ They emphasise processes of change in the form of religious organisations and stress the importance of social development in the evolution of any specific organisation.
+ The concept of the 'cult' allows an exploration of some of the more negative aspects of religious organisations.
− Not all sects believe in the values of thrift. Therefore, there is no necessary process of becoming wealthy and upwardly mobile, thus creating the impetus towards a denomination.
− Many sects, for example the Jehovah's Witnesses, far from being led by charismatic and inspirational leaders, are very bureaucratic, so routinisation cannot be claimed as a feature of becoming a denomination.
− The idea of the cult creates a stereotype of religious organisations that can be used to criticise the activities of any of them.

Key concepts

formalism, inspirationalism, baptism, non-universalism, mysticism

Key thinkers

Niebuhr, von Weise, Wallis

More complex views of religious organisation

Key ideas

- The range of religious organisations is much larger than the four-fold divisions of church, sect, denomination and cult suggested by many typologies.

Knowledge check 13

Give an example of a contemporary cult.

Examiner tip

Be active in your revision strategies — don't just sit there and read your notes. Try to do exercises and activities that test your AO2 skills.

Knowledge check 14

Give one example of where the Roman Catholic Church has been conservative and one where it has been radical.

- In addition, the role of any religious organisation cannot be said to be either conservative or radical at all times, but varies according to which level of the organisation is examined, the cultural and historical context within which it operates, as well as the nature of its beliefs.
- 'Universal church' refers to a dominant religious form that is cross-national and operates independently of individual political units. An example is Roman Catholicism before the Reformation.
- An ecclesia refers to a religion that is identifiable as the state religion of a specific nation-state, such as Shia Islam in Iran.
- An established sect refers to a long-lived sect that has made an accommodation with the state over most issues, but remains opposed to the state on certain specifics. The pacifism of the Quaker movement is an example.
- Sects can take many forms and can be classified according to their attitude towards the secular world. They may accept it as a something to be lived with and celebrated, or avoid the world completely, or be actively opposed and hostile to the secular powers.
- Sects can be further divided into many different types, from the conversionist, evangelical, fundamentalist sects to **thaumaturgical sects** that seek contact with a spirit world.
- The relationship of any religious organisation to the world is complex, and each empirical example needs to be examined separately rather than stereotypically.

Thaumaturgical sects
These promise their members that they will gain material advantages through contact with the spiritual world.

Examiner tip
Practise 'real' exam questions as often as you can. Look at the answers in this unit guide and use them as exemplars and for improving your own performance.

Evaluation

+ These complex typologies offer a more complete understanding of the nature of religious organisations.
+ They put forward a more dynamic view of the way that religious organisations operate in the world.
+ They suggest that religious organisations are subject to processes of change, as well as rooted in tradition.
- All these typologies can be criticised for focusing mainly on Christian organisations and ignoring or downplaying the other major world religions.
- Complex typologies can become so convoluted that they cease to have any explanatory power.
- The examples used to support particular typologies can often be based on a stereotypical view of the real religious life of organisations.

Key concepts
universal church, ecclesia, established sect, acceptance, aggression, avoidance

Key thinkers
Yinger, Wilson, Maguire

New Religious Movements

Key ideas

- 'New Religious Movements' (NRMs) is a term used to describe the many forms of religious groups that have emerged throughout the world, separate from the traditional forms of world religions, but often related to them.
- World-rejecting NRMs, such as Krishna Consciousness, are inward-looking and strict organisations that tend to avoid contact with outsiders as far as possible, in the search for spiritual enlightenment.
- World-affirming NRMs, such as Scientology, see success in the secular world as one of the aims of their spiritual journey within it.
- World-accommodating NRMs, such as Neo-Pentecostalism, are outward-looking, tolerant and charismatic movements.
- Some NRMs are accused of using brain-washing techniques and isolation of members from their families as a means of control, and can be associated with a charismatic leader, at whose command members will even take their own life.
- NRMs are believed to emerge during times of social change and are often seen as perfect for the postmodern era with its loss of certainty, in offering those in search of answers a 'true' account of the world.
- NRMs are said to offer recruits success in careers, improved health and self-development and 'authentic' religious experience, through 'client cults' and 'self-religions'.
- NRMs are often difficult to leave, partly because of the psychological investment that has been made in them, but also because the usual social ties may have been cut and continuing members may be hostile to the leaver.
- There has been much media attention on the 'doomsday' NRMs, whose members engage in acts of suicide (Jonesville) or terror (Aum Shinrikyo).
- A particular form of NRM is the political coalition of fundamentalist Christian groups in the USA (New Christian Right), which seek to impose their beliefs on the rest of society by influencing the president.
- New Age Movements, such as paganism, Gaia and astrology, are also seen as a form of alternative NRM, with a focus on inner spirituality, the environment, and forms of spiritualism and Eastern mysticism.

Charisma A quality in an individual that attracts others to them by the force of his or her personality.

Knowledge check 15

Identify a contemporary political movement in the USA that draws upon fundamentalist religious belief and free market economics.

Examiner tip

Organise your revision so that you are not trying to do it all in the few nights before the exam. You need to sleep well the night before.

Evaluation

- + 'New Religious Movement', as a wider term than sect or cult, is a more appropriate way of defining the many religious groups that emerged in the latter part of the twentieth century.
- + NRMs have introduced a revival of religious feeling and devotion in many societies, and have attracted those who might otherwise be turned off from mainstream religion.
- + NRMs have had a positive effect on the mainstream Christian church in introducing charismatic behaviour and worship into traditional congregations.

- There is wide variation in NRMs, and many do not fit easily into the various categories proposed, nor do they emerge only in times of instability.
- NRMs are stereotyped as being 'dangerous' and controlling, when they may offer members reassurance and control over their own lives.
- NRMs are nothing new, as there have always been subterranean religious forms. However, in the past they were more likely to be criticised or even suppressed for being heretical.

Key concepts

world-affirming, world-rejecting, world-accommodating, charismatic, New Age, New Christian Right, client cults

Key thinkers

Wallis, Barker, Beckford, Davie, Bruce, Heelas

Summary

- Traditionally, religious organisations have been associated with their attitude towards the state and were simply divided into churches and sects.
- As sociologists recognised differences between religious organisations, new categories, such as denominations and cults arose.

- Ever more complex typologies have been developed that seek to characterise religious organisations comprehensively.
- A distinction is increasingly drawn between traditional religious organisations that have long-established histories and New Religious Movements that are often the result of mixing together religious ideas from different traditions.

Religion and social groups

Religion and class

Key ideas

Dominant social class In Marxist terms, in capitalism, this is the bourgeoisie or the owners of the means of production.

- From a Marxist perspective, religion has been seen as functioning as an ideology in defence of the interests of the dominant social class in society.
- Interest theorists argue that religious ideas are a weapon in the struggle for advantage between different social groups and a mask for real social and economic conflicts.
- Strain theorists argue that religions emerge as a result of social dislocation and personal tensions and function to resolve these tensions (catharsis) in ways that are advantageous to those who adhere to them, from providing a scapegoat for unpleasant events in symbolic evil to legitimating strain in terms of a higher being.

The strains that may be resolved by religion are not only economic, but also social (in terms of lack of power or esteem), organismic (mental or physical impairment), psychic (anomie) and ethical (dissatisfaction with society's values).

- At the base of these theories is the fact that different social classes profess allegiance to different forms of religion, even within a broad world religion; for example, Shia Islam draws recruits mainly from among the poorer sections of Afghanistan.
- In Great Britain, the Church of England is dominated by a middle-class membership as it fails to recruit among the urbanised working classes.
- Some Protestant denominations, as well as Islam, Sikhism and Hinduism, find strong support in the working classes.
- Sects are sometimes seen as recruiting mainly from the disadvantaged in society, as they seek to resolve the tensions such people experience.
- Central to the appeal of religions are their 'theodices of good and ill fortune', that is the explanations for suffering or success, that legitimate the position of those who experience either.
- Religion is, therefore, a consequence of 'compensators' — the belief that reward for living a 'good life' will be obtained in the future, either on earth or in some form of heaven.

Knowledge check 16

Identify one Protestant organisation that has recruited mainly among working-class individuals.

Evaluation

+ There is a class basis for many religious organisations and this has been explained through concepts such as compensators.
+ There is a link between world-affirming sects and the advantaged in society, and world-rejecting sects and the poor. This shows the importance of exploring the class nature of NRMs.
+ There are strong religious feelings among all social classes that express themselves in different ways and in different organisations.
- Sects are not just havens for the poor and dissatisfied, but also recruit from the rich and those who seemingly have everything.
- The statistical link between class and different types of sect is uncertain, especially because there are so few members of sects and cults.
- The appeal of religion is not universal among social classes and most individuals do not formally align to any religious organisation in contemporary Britain.

Examiner tip

Use the internet. There are some excellent sites dedicated to A-level sociology and more general sociological sites that will stretch your sociological imagination.

Key concepts

ideology, catharsis, solidarity, compensators

Key thinkers

Geertz, Glock and Stark, Stark and Bainbridge, Voas, Wallis

Religion and gender

Key ideas

- Many ancient religions had strong female images in the form of goddesses, but these have mainly been supplanted by male-dominated monotheistic religions such as Judaism, Christianity and Islam.
- The major religions therefore tend to privilege maleness in their theology, beliefs and practices.
- Where women are represented in religious beliefs, they tend to be in a submissive role or as agents of evil or temptation.
- Religious organisations are mainly male-led, especially at the higher levels, with the position of priest being barred to females in some major religions.
- Where females are allowed to take positions of authority or sacramental roles, it is only after long and protracted struggles by female (and male) adherents.
- Many religions seek to restrict the behaviour of women, emphasising modesty and submission to male authority. This can have a physical expression in the separation of male and female worshippers during religious services.
- Religions are often hostile to overt sexuality and see the control of women as essential to control the libido.
- Debates over the role of women in religion are seen as an argument between 'modernisers' and 'traditionalists', with the former often accused of being secular contaminators of 'pure' forms of religion.
- Outward religious forms for women are often presented in Western societies as symbolic of the 'Other', for example the wearing of the veil (hijab) by Muslim women.
- Yet, in many religions, women form the majority of regular attenders at services.
- In science, women's role in discovery has often been ignored or downplayed, such as Rosalind Franklin's contribution to the discovery of DNA.
- In New Age movements, a gender divide can be identified in the types of movements women and men are attracted to, with women favouring areas such as complementary medicine and men leaning towards parapsychology.

Evaluation

- + Women and men are claimed to have different natures and therefore the different roles within religion for men and women are 'natural'.
- + Religious recognition of the differences between men and women has been strongly held by many ordinary believers over a long period of time.
- + There is a tradition of male domination, going back to the founders of the major religions, that says that it should be followed, as it is a result of divine instruction.
- − Many women willingly accept the different role from men that religion requires them to play, seeing the gender hierarchy as a God-given duty for womenkind.
- − Many religions have 'liberal' strands within them that stress equality between the genders in the eyes of God.
- − Women are increasingly making inroads into positions of religious authority; for example, the acceptance of female priests in the Church of England.

Knowledge check 17

What is meant by theology in the sociology of belief?

Libido The sexual drive in humans.

Examiner tip

Subscribe to *Sociology Review* and access back copies held by your school or college library. It is one of the best sources of contemporary sociological work in the areas you will be examined on.

Key concepts

patriarchy, monotheism, sexuality, ordination of women

Key thinkers

El Saadawi, McGuire, Barker, Aldridge

Religion and ethnic identity

Key ideas

- 'Identity' has three components: the knowledge that one belongs to a group; the positive or negative values of belonging to a group; and the emotional attachment to a group or distance from other groups.
- Religious identity is therefore the knowledge, values and feelings relating to membership of a religious minority or majority in a society.
- Religion is one of the basic building blocks of ethnic identity, alongside nationality, shared history, language and assumptions about the 'body' (for example genetic inheritance).
- Ethnic identities are multidimensional and also interpenetrative. For example, British Muslims have a shared identity across these dimensions, with a national identity as British citizens, values as members of a British Muslim community and perhaps feelings of belonging to a global Ummah (community of believers).
- Religion provides individuals with many 'markers' of identity, such as customs, dress, food, rituals, celebrations etc., but these are often fluid rather than rigid, e.g. fusion cuisine.
- Religion may also prove a powerful marker of ethnic identity because it can be a means of dealing with 'bafflement', allowing minorities to make sense of their position in society and of discrimination that they may experience.
- In postmodern societies, the fluidity of social relations and the lack of a solid identity in an urban landscape infused with myriad cultures can lead to a turning back to religion as a source of community — the formation of 'neo-tribes'.
- Postmodern uncertainties of identity affect majorities as well as minorities, and Christian as well as non-Christian religious expression.

Body In sociology, this does not just mean the physical aspects of our appearance, but also refers to the way that we think about our bodies and how they shape the way that others respond to us.

Knowledge check 18

What do sociologists call these multidimensional identities?

Evaluation

- + This approach locates religious identity within a set of other sources of identity, but shows the importance of religious belief for marginalised groups in society.
- + It offers a dynamic and open view of identity as not fixed in a traditional formation but as adaptive to the realities of postmodern living.
- + It helps to explain the persistence of religious attachment among certain sections of the population within a generally more secular society.
- − Some versions of identity theory fall into 'primordialism', that is, they argue that ethnic communities are 'natural' and exclusivist.

Examiner tip

Watch television and films from a sociological point of view and try to apply appropriate concepts to the stories. This will develop the skill of application.

- Identity theory can overemphasise the attachment of young members of ethnic minorities in particular to religious belief, rather than the forms of religious behaviour, as a marker of identity.
- It can assume that ethnic majorities are more secular than ethnic minorities because of their majority position, which means they take their identity for granted.

Key concepts

social identity, Ummah, primordialism, neo-tribes

Key thinkers

Tafjel, Nash, Geertz, Berger, Bauman

Religion and fundamentalism

Key ideas

- Fundamentalism is the strict assertion of the basic beliefs of a religion, often expressed as a belief in the literal truth of the holy book of a religion.
- It can be seen more broadly as a conservative interpretation of faith, in which there is an emphasis on traditional values while the techniques of modernity are accepted as a means of spreading the conservative message.
- Fundamentalism can also be seen as a response by religious individuals and groups to the uncertainties of the postmodern world, with an emphasis on knowing the truth as revealed by their god, and by which they lead their lives.
- While using modern techniques of propaganda, fundamentalism is a profound rejection of modernity and seeks to impose its vision of a holy state on the whole of society.
- It is expressed in different ways in different religions, from the traditional dress of Ultra-Orthodox Jews, who reject the Israeli state, to the jihadis of the Taliban who controlled Afghanistan from 1996 to 2001, the terrorists of al-Qaeda and the New Christian Right political movement in the USA.
- Certain issues become **talismanic** for fundamentalist beliefs, such as opposition to abortion for some Christians or the wearing of the chador for women under strict Islamic rules.
- What unites all fundamentalists is their dislike of secularism and the liberal consensus of the Western world, which they view as responsible for disorder, crime and sinfulness.
- Education is often a key battleground for fundamentalist groups, whether it concerns the teaching of creationism or intelligent design by the Christian Right or the right of Islamic women to wear the veil under French educational laïcité. The growth of fundamentalist schools is an important political issue.
- Fundamentalists across many religions are united in an anti-homosexual attitude, ranging from opposition to gay marriage in the USA to the public hanging of gay men in Iran.

Knowledge check 19

Identify one feature of modernity.

Talisman A 'marker out', something that helps to distinguish the religious from the secular.

● In Islam, the growth of fundamentalist belief is associated with the domination of the West over the Muslim world and an anti-Americanism which sees the USA as the 'Great Satan'.

Examiner tip
Try to read a quality newspaper regularly. They are useful for practising applying your sociological skills to contemporary news stories and for picking up examples to use in the examination.

Evaluation

+ The growth of fundamentalist organisations has been prolific and can perhaps be explained as a reaction against postmodernity, in which all metanarratives have been undermined.

+ The events of 11 September 2001 illustrate the challenge of fundamentalism and its claim to be treated as a serious development in religion.

+ Fundamentalism represents an authentic religious response through recalling an era of true religiosity.

– Fundamentalism was born out of the Christian religion and is not easily translated to the other world religions, especially Islam, where the Qur'an is seen as literally the word of God by all Muslims.

– It is uncertain how far fundamentalism has actually grown. As the most vocal of religious groups, fundamentalists tend to dominate religious discourse and drown out the voice of the moderate religious majority.

– Different societies have various responses to the perceived growth of fundamentalism, from political accommodation (the USA under the Republicans) to opposition (Algeria).

Key concepts

literalism, laïcité, talismanic, fundamentalism

Key thinkers

Kepel, Bruce, Modood, Gellner

● The relationship between religious organisations and different social groups is complex and often full of conflict.

● Religious organisations can be distinguished by the social class membership of their adherents as they have different appeals to people in different social groupings.

● The place of women within religious groups is often problematic, in that they are denied positions in the higher echelons of the organisation, on account of tradition.

● Religion is a key marker of identity among many ethnic minority groups and acts as a focus for groups in marginalised positions.

● The emergence of fundamentalist religions is a feature of postmodern societies and poses a challenge both to orthodox religion and to secularists.

Summary

Secularisation

What is secularisation?

Key ideas

- Many early theorists were hostile to religion and saw its decline as inevitable as reason and science explained what had previously been subject to religious dogma.
- The definition of religion affects whether secularisation can be said to have happened or not. Exclusivist definitions tend to involve secularisation as 'pure' forms of religion evolve to respond to social changes. Inclusivist definitions, meanwhile, assume that there will always be some form of religion in society as it is essential for the maintenance of good relationships between members.
- The quantum theory of religion suggests that part of human nature is an innate religiosity, which means that religious forms or expressions may change, but religion in one form or another is always with us.
- Secularists believe that there is a logic to history that leads people and societies increasingly to reject religious forms and instead embrace non-religious ideas and behaviours.
- The rationalisation of society, according to Weber, means that people put aside tradition and charisma in favour of reason and science.
- Shiner argues that secularisation has been used by sociologists in at least six different ways, employing as many definitions.
- An overarching definition of secularisation would therefore be 'the loss of influence of religion over society and over individuals'.

Evaluation

- + The definition of secularisation is an important issue because it determines the way that sociologists try to measure it.
- + It is vital to know exactly what is being studied so that sociologists can explore the phenomenon rigorously.
- + Without the concept of secularisation, it would be difficult to examine social change in religious habits and beliefs.
- − Definitions can cut off areas of exploration as well as open them up.
- − Definitions of secularisation are built up on pre-existing beliefs about the importance of religion. Those who see religion as essential do not accept that secularisation has occurred at all.
- − There have been many sociological studies focusing on how to define secularisation rather than exploring the empirical reality of religious behaviour.

Key concepts

secularisation, charisma, rationalisation, science

Exclusivist definitions
These refer to spirituality/God as an essential part of a religion.

Inclusivist definitions
These refer to any system of belief that seeks to make sense of the world, regardless of whether it mentions God or not.

Knowledge check 20
What is meant by the term 'innate'?

Examiner tip
Use the internet independently but *carefully* to find out about contemporary examples and current developments in sociology.

Key thinkers

Weber, Wilson, Shiner, Robertson, Beckford

Secularisation and society

Key ideas

- The basic notion in looking at society and religion is drawn from Wilson's view that religion 'loses its social significance'.
- This implies that previously well-accepted religious symbols and institutions become less important and lose their status in society.
- This can occur in several ways, such as atrophy or bureaucratisation or the loss of religious thought as a guide to action.
- The process began in Christianity with the Reformation, which introduced choice into religious belief from the unitary world of medieval Catholicism. Choice reduces religion to servicing the needs of distinctive interest groups rather than embodying a whole society.
- The process is called societalisation and is where personal ties are replaced by contractual bonds between individuals, such that the role of the priest as a personal advocate for the individual with God is lost.
- Secular societies welcome social change, while religious societies are resistant. It is therefore the cities, the forges of change, that are the centre of the de-Christianisation of society.
- Religion therefore retreats into the private sphere and loses its public prominence, although vestiges may remain, such as the position of the bishops of the Church of England in the House of Lords.
- This process involves a loss of social status for the clergy and a reduction in the economic power of the church, with a subsequent decline in the proportion of the GDP that is spent on spiritual matters.
- The roles performed by the church are also depleted as societies industrialise and specialised secular agencies emerge to carry out functions originally performed by the church, such as ministering to the poor.
- This loss of functions for the church is accompanied by a shift among the churches to a 'this-worldly' orientation, using advertising techniques to attract adherents and forming unions among small denominations to combat declining attendance.
- Ecumenicalism is therefore a sign of structural weakness rather than a revival of true religious feeling.

> **Bureaucratisation**
> The process whereby an organisation becomes more concerned with the administration of things than with the achievement of its goals.

> **Knowledge check 21**
> Give another example of where religious organisations have been replaced by secular equivalents.

Evaluation

- + There has clearly been some decline in the power of the church to influence social policies and historical events in Western societies.
- + Structural differentiation is a feature of modernisation and inevitably involves some loss of functions for religious institutions.

+ The economic and social decline of religious institutions has a physical manifestation in the deconsecration and sale of redundant churches.
- These approaches presuppose a 'golden age of religion', in which there was one dominant religious organisation. Even at the height of Catholic domination of Europe, the church was riven by disputes, heretical movements and subterranean theologies.
- There is a difference between formal attendance at church for social reasons and for the purpose of worship. It may be that there never was any golden age of belief (as opposed to social attendance) from which a decline has occurred.
- The extent to which formal religious institutions have lost power varies from society to society and it may be a Western phenomenon, not paralleled, for example, in Islamic societies.

Key concepts

atrophy, bureaucratisation, societalisation, loss of functions, structural differentiation

Key thinkers

Wilson, Shiner, Berger, Parsons

Religious practices

Key ideas

- At the level of culture, it is argued that there has been a shift of beliefs and behaviour away from a religious or spiritual frame of reference towards a secular frame.
- An example of this shift is the emergence of 'secular' or 'civil' religions, where there are outward signs of religious behaviour but in relation to secular objects. The ideology of Marxism is often cited as an example, with its 'saints', 'icons' and metaphysical belief in a better world.
- These secular beliefs are functional equivalents of religion in a postmodern world and constitute a surrogate religiosity.
- There is also a decline in the observance of religious forms, as measured in a number of ways:
  - There is a drop in the formal membership of the major churches, which is not offset by a rise in those who belong to the more marginal religious groupings.
  - The church is used less frequently for rites of passage such as baptism, marriage and funerals, with the latter still being the most 'popular' use of the church's facilities.
  - There is a fall in the number of people who attend church on either a regular or an occasional basis.
  - Regular Sunday attendance has dropped, as has observance of major festivals such as Christmas, which are more secular than ever before.
  - The growth in alternative forms of entertainment such as television and the internet has led to a fall off in, for example, Sunday school attendance.

Knowledge check 22

What is meant by a 'surrogate religiosity'?

- There has been a growth in religious pluralism which has altered the way that individuals practise their beliefs. For example, the growing House Church movement stands outside the traditional churches and is not taken into account in the official statistics for attendance.
- However, the element of choice implicit in religious pluralism suggests a fragmentation of religious behaviour and the potential for individuals to move between religious institutions during their life course.
- Many sects with growing membership are said to be only superficially religious and to function more as religious surrogates, being aimed at secular success rather than representing a return to real religiosity.

> **House Church movement** This takes its name from the fact that groups of believers meet in each other's houses rather than in church buildings.

Evaluation

+ There is a consistent trend, year on year, towards fewer instances of religious observance, however measured.
+ Rituals and symbols need not have a religious dimension, but may fulfil a human need for pageantry and spectacle rather than a fundamental religiosity.
+ The shift towards secular forms of rites of passage is significant and is reflected in changing legislation, for example that which allows the performance of the marriage ceremony in any licensed location.
- The issue of US exceptionalism is important here. The decline in religious observance has not occurred to the same extent in the USA as it has in Europe. This undermines claims for a general global secularisation.
- There is relatively little decline in the numbers who claim some affiliation to the major religions, and an increase in the numbers who align with sectarian and other forms of religious behaviour.
- There are methodological problems with collecting statistics on attendance and belief that make such statistics suspect and inconclusive.

> **Examiner tip**
> In the exam, divide your time appropriately for the number of marks and make sure that you attempt all parts of a question asked.

Key concepts

secular religions, surrogate religiosity, exceptionalism

Key thinkers

Robertson, Bellah, Wilson

Religious consciousness

Key ideas

- Modernity is characterised by a growth in rationality and the disenchantment of the world. This involves individuals discarding myth, charm and poetry to embrace scientific explanations.
- There has been a decline in belief in magic and superstition as natural phenomena become subject to scientific scrutiny.

> **Knowledge check 23**
> Which classical sociologist used the phrase 'the end of myth, charm and poetry' to describe secularisation?

- The ideology of science has permeated the consciousness of individuals and set up oppositions to irrational beliefs.
- One response of the religious community has been the growth of 'rational' religions that seek to reconcile scientificity with a belief in God. Rational religion is often counterposed to the growth of fundamentalist thinking.
- As the community of believers becomes smaller under the impact of industrialisation, the plausibility structure of religious belief (the institutions and networks that make belief in the irrational possible) is threatened.
- Surveys still show a high proportion of the population who profess a belief in a supernatural being, although the nature of the transcendental being is not always in accordance with traditional religious beliefs.
- As Christianity retreats from the public sphere, the young are much more likely to 'believe without belonging'.
- Knowledge of orthodox religious doctrine is low, as is familiarity with the major text(s) of the religion to which people express an affiliation.
- It is claimed that religious ideas about morality have less of a hold over people's ideas and behaviour as they turn away from religious morality altogether or adopt secular alternatives.
- This is often manifested in the disjunction between the teachings of the church and the behaviour of those who claim strong allegiance to it, for example over birth control.
- Britain could be described as 'post-Christian', with people identifying with some traditional values, such as kindness, but rejecting others, such as sexual Puritanism.

Orthodox religious doctrine The official and formal beliefs of a religious organisation rather than what its members actually believe.

Evaluation

+ The growth in crime and anti-social behaviour is claimed to be the result of the loss of influence of religious morality over individual behaviour.
+ The unpopularity of religious education in schools and the decline in Sunday school attendance result in a lack of exposure to religious ideas among children.
+ Religious festivals, such as Christmas, are increasingly used as secular holidays rather than events imbued with religious meaning.
− Scientific belief-systems cannot provide answers to ultimate questions and thus there will always be a search for the deeper reasons for existence.
− There is still a large reservoir of belief in the subterranean theologies of magic and superstition, as demonstrated by the belief in astrology etc.
− Polling information suggests that the impact of religion on individual consciousness may have diffused, but it still has a strong pull on people's consciences.

Examiner tip
Read the questions on the examination paper carefully to ensure that you are writing relevantly.

Key concepts

disenchantment, plausibility structure, Gods of the Gaps, believing without belonging

Key thinkers

Berger, Wilson, Shiner, Woodhead

Anti-secularisation

Key ideas

- Secularisation theory is accused of being based on a teleological assumption; that is, it is a product of a Marxist/rationalist ideology which holds that, as societies modernise, they will get rid of old-fashioned ideas such as religion.
- Secularisation is therefore built on the back of a simplified view of history as a set of dualisms, in which religious/secular is affixed to traditional/modern.
- Rather than being an objective view of the development of societies, secularism represents an ideology that is unremitting in its hostility to all religious forms.
- Secularisation underestimates the diversity of different patterns of religious behaviour and thought under the conditions of modernity and postmodernity.
- Moreover, it is an ethnocentric view of religious developments, dismissing the persistence of religion in less economically developed countries as a result of their lack of modernity.
- Even in its own terms, secularisation theory does not hold true, as evidenced by the power of religious organisations in contemporary US society and the growth in sects.
- Rather than a decline in religion, society is seeing the growth of a 'new voluntarism' in religion, in which people have choices to make in a self-conscious reflexive process that might result in individuals continuing in the faith of their birth or joining a new form.
- Rational choice theory suggests that humans will always seek out a meaning to life and they make their religious choices by balancing the costs and benefits of adopting a particular belief system.
- In this sense we are religious consumers, calculating the cost of being committed to a particular set of rules and activities and setting this against the promised benefit of redemption.
- Our choices are made on the basis of different forms of religious commitment: the communal (to a community of believers), the ethical (to a belief-system), the cultural (to texts and traditions) and the emotional (to intensity of expression).

Knowledge check 24

What is meant by 'ethnocentric'?

Reflexivity When we, as individuals, think back on our actions and ideas and reflect on them in order to make changes or to confirm what we already know and do.

Evaluation

- + There is no inevitable decline in religion, rather religious observance varies across time and space and form.
- + The growth of non-standard religious institutions, such as fundamentalist sects, suggests that a religious revival is occurring, negating the secularisation thesis.
- + The development of rational choice theory offers an alternative way of explaining the empirical developments that have taken place.
- − The emergence of new religious forms and the need to choose between them can be seen as a fragmentation of religion into a weakened and marginalised set of institutions.
- − Secularisation theory is not just concerned with a dualistic view of history, but attempts to explain a complex and multifaceted phenomenon.

Examiner tip
Ensure that you include all elements of the skills required by the question in your answer.

– It is difficult to apply the concept of rational individual choice to such an irrational form as religion.

Key concepts

consumerism, rational choice, religious commitment

Key thinkers

Martin, Wilson, Herberg, Bruce, Stark and Bainbridge, Hervieu-Léger, Holden

Summary

- Secularisation is not easy to define as there have been so many attempts to do so.
- Secularists claim that religious influence over society as a whole has declined and this is a consequence of the influence of modernity on society.
- Religious practices have changed greatly in modern/postmodern societies, with a decline in formal attendance at religious services.
- Religious belief still seems to be relatively strong in modern/postmodern societies, though it is not clear what those religious beliefs actually are.
- Secularisation has come under attack for ignoring much evidence for the durability of religious beliefs and practices rather than their decline.

Questions & Answers

How to use this section

In this section, there are four sets of sample questions on the topic of Beliefs in Society. Each question is followed by a brief analysis of what to watch out for when answering it (shown by the icon ⓔ). The questions are followed by specimen student answers, with examiner's comments (preceded by the icon ⓔ). Try to answer the questions first yourself, and then use the sample answers and examiner's comments for guidance. Remember that in the actual exam, you will be given a choice for the long essay questions (03 or 04). In these examples, only one such question is provided.

It is important to note that the way in which the students have answered the questions represents only *one* appropriate way. You may be able to think of different examples for the shorter questions, and other ways of approaching the longer essay questions.

Examinable skills

A2 Sociology papers are designed to test certain defined skills. These skills are expressed as assessment objectives in the AQA specification. You will have been tested on these assessment objectives in your AS Sociology unit examinations, but the weighting for each of the two assessment objectives (AO1 and AO2) is different for the A2 Sociology specification. Over the two units of A2, the proportion of marks given to AO1 (knowledge and understanding) is just over 40% and for AO2 (application, analysis, interpretation and evaluation), it is about 58%. The effect of this is that, at A2, you have to be able to demonstrate more sophisticated skills of analysis and evaluation than at AS. You will be required to show a more critical, reflective and evaluative approach to methodological issues, to the nature of sociological enquiry and to sociological debates, drawing on a broad and diverse range of sources.

Unit 3 constitutes 20% of the total marks available for the whole of AS and A2, but the assessment objective weighting for Unit 3 is 40% for AO1 skills and 60% for AO2 skills. This shows the proportion of marks allocated to each of the two assessment objectives. Three-fifths of the 60 marks available in the Unit 3 examination are therefore awarded to the demonstration of AO2 skills and only two-fifths to AO1 skills.

Assessment objective 1 (AO1): knowledge and understanding

AO1 concerns the paired skills of knowledge and understanding. You have to demonstrate clearly to the examiners that you have appropriate, accurate knowledge and a good understanding of the sociological material in the topic you are studying. The Content guidance section of this guide provides an account of the basic knowledge required for Beliefs in Society. The reason for bringing together knowledge and understanding is that it is not enough to be able to reproduce in the exam knowledge learned by rote. You must also be able to use this knowledge in a meaningful way to answer the specific question set. This includes the ability to select the most appropriate information from the range of knowledge that you have.

In addition, you have to demonstrate your knowledge and understanding of the **core themes** of the specification. These are:

- socialisation, culture and identity
- social differentiation, power and stratification

Aspects of these themes are dealt with in various elements of the AS and A2 courses. The themes therefore run through the whole of the course and this includes the topic of Beliefs in Society. The Content guidance section of this guide provides examples of where these themes are dealt with.

Each topic in sociology, including Beliefs in Society, also has to cover what are called **integral elements**, that is, information and approaches that are central to sociology and that are found in all the topics studied at Advanced level. The integral elements cover:

- sociological theories, perspectives and methods
- the design and evaluation of research methods

Therefore, one of the demands of the AQA specification for AS and A2 Sociology is that you have a good knowledge and understanding of a range of sociological methods and sources and that, in particular, you understand the relationship between theory and methods. This includes the way that sociologists:

- acquire primary and secondary data through observation, asking questions and using documents
- analyse qualitative and quantitative data using appropriate concepts
- take into account factors influencing the design and conduct of sociological research
- are influenced by practical, ethical and theoretical considerations

The nature of sociological thought is concerned with both concepts and sociological theories. A requirement of the specification is that you make the links between these concepts and theories and the substantive area you have chosen to study — in this case, Beliefs in Society. The nature of sociological thought covers:

- social order, social control
- social change
- conflict and consensus
- social structure and social action
- the role of values
- the relationship between sociology and contemporary social policy

The final part of the AO1 skills requirement concerns the quality of written communication. This includes the ability to:

- use a style of writing appropriate for transmitting complex information
- use specialist vocabulary, such as sociological concepts, when appropriate
- use accurate spelling, punctuation and grammar to ensure that the meaning is clear and the text is legible

Assessment objective 2 (AO2): application, analysis, interpretation and evaluation

AO2 covers application, analysis, interpretation and evaluation. At A2 you need to be more critical and evaluative than in the AS exams, as more marks are given to AO2 skills than to AO1 skills.

You will, therefore, need to:

- select appropriate pieces of sociological knowledge and arguments and distinguish between facts and opinion (**application**)
- break down sociological studies and debates into their component parts, i.e. concepts, perspective, method, findings, conclusion, strengths and weaknesses (**analysis**)
- examine material such as statistics, tables, graphs, research findings etc. to identify trends and establish their meaning and importance (**interpretation**)
- assess the relevance and importance of sociological studies and debates, conveying their strengths and weaknesses and coming to a conclusion about them (**evaluation**)

Evaluation is a particularly important skill at A2. In practice, this means that you should be asking questions such as, 'Why should I believe this?', 'What evidence is there for this viewpoint?', 'Are there any counter-arguments?' and 'Who says so?' for every piece of sociological research or approach that you come across. Try to develop the habit of evaluation as you go through your course. A good way to do this is to establish a minimum of two strengths and two weaknesses for every piece of research or every point of view or sociological perspective that you examine. It is even better if you can come to a conclusion about whether every item is convincing or not, with your conclusion backed by rational argument and solid sociological research.

As well as the above skills, AO2 includes the ability to:

- organise your arguments coherently
- display an understanding of theoretical debates in sociology
- marshal evidence to support arguments and any conclusions you make

The unit test

Beliefs in Society is a Unit 3 topic. The unit also contains the topics of Global Development, Mass Media, and Power and Politics. It is unlikely that you will have covered more than one of these topics in your course, but, if you have, you must choose only *one* of the four sections on the examination paper. Beliefs in Society is Section A. It is worth 20% of the entire A-level qualification and is therefore an important component.

Within Section A, you have to answer two compulsory questions (01 and 02). There are then two essay questions and you must choose only one of these (question 03 or 04).

Attached to questions 01 and 02 will be a single item of source material. This is designed to help you by providing information on which you may draw to answer question 01 and/or question 02. You should read this material carefully, *before* attempting to answer the questions. It may provide you with important clues in answering one or both of the parts. When one of the questions refers specifically to the source material ('Using Item A' or 'With reference to Item A and elsewhere'), you are *required* to make use of the source material. You should do this as obviously as possible to assist the marker in identifying where in your answer you have obeyed the instruction. For example, you might write:

'As Item A demonstrates...'

'The view in Item A suggests a functionalist approach is most useful...'

Timing and mark allocation

Unit 3 Section A questions are worth 60 marks in total, with 9 marks given to question 01, 18 marks to question 02 and 33 marks to either question 03 or question 04, depending on which you choose.

The division of marks between the elements you have to answer (9, 18 and 33) indicates the time that you should allocate to each element. As you have 1 hour and 30 minutes, you should devote roughly half of the time to question 03 or question 04 (about 50 minutes), about 20 minutes to question 02 and about 10 minutes to question 01, leaving 5 minutes for reading through the item of source material and 5 minutes reviewing at the end.

As we have seen, 40% of the marks in Unit 3 as a whole are given to AO1 skills and 60% to AO2 skills. There is some variation within this, however. In questions 03 and 04, the balance of AO1 and AO2 marks is nearly equal — 15 marks for AO1 and 18 marks for AO2. In questions 01 and 02, AO2 marks are in the majority. For question 01, AO1 is given 3 marks and AO2 6 marks. For question 02, AO1 is given 6 marks and AO2 12 marks. A further complication is that, in the longer essay questions (questions 03 and 04), the AO2 marks are subdivided equally between AO2 (a), interpretation and application and AO2 (b), analysis and evaluation, with 9 marks for each.

The important thing to note in all this is that the skills of interpretation, application, analysis and evaluation are more important in A2 examinations than they are at AS, and therefore you must take care to demonstrate them. Pay particular attention to the wording of questions, which provides you with clues as to the particular skills being asked for. Remember also that you need to provide evidence of knowledge and understanding of material from Beliefs in Society, so do not neglect this skill either.

Example 1 Church attendance; young people and belief; functions of religion

Read Item A below and answer questions 01 and 02 that follow. Then answer question 03.

Item A

Church attendance has been in rapid decline in recent decades, with young people less and less likely to be regular church-goers. In studies such as the annual British Social Attitudes Survey, more than half of them say that they regard themselves as not being religious. Yet at the same time, for some young people, religion is a profoundly important part of their lives. So on the one hand, we see growing numbers of young people disengaging from religion, and on the other hand, an increasing intensity of religious devotion among a minority of young people.

Other factors have made this picture of change more complex. For example, since the 1960s, Western societies have seen the emergence of what the sociologist Wade Clark Roof calls an 'expanded spiritual marketplace'. There has been a significant opening up of religious identities, beliefs and activities from the possibilities offered by traditional religious institutions.

Source: adapted from G. Lynch (2007), 'Understanding the sacred', *Sociology Review*, Vol. 17, No. 2.

(01) Identify and briefly explain *three* problems with using church attendance statistics to measure the extent of religious belief   (9 marks)

ⓔ This type of question carries 3 marks for each of the three problems identified and briefly explained. The usual format is to allow 1 mark for something correctly identified, and up to 2 further marks for the quality and accuracy of the explanation. It is helpful to separate out the three parts of your answer, either by leaving a blank line or by using bullet points. While your answer should be sufficiently detailed to gain all the marks, do not be tempted to write more than is necessary — you will be losing valuable time from the higher-mark questions.

(02) Using material from Item A and elsewhere, examine the reasons why some young people may show 'an increasing intensity of religious devotion' (Item A).   (18 marks)

ⓔ Here you are asked to 'examine the reasons' — obviously, you should be able to come up with more than one. Although 'examine' as a command word is not as strong on evaluation as 'assess' or 'evaluate', 12 of the 18 marks available are allotted to AO2 skills — application, analysis, interpretation and evaluation, so your answer needs to display these.

(03) Assess the view that religion still performs important functions for society.   (33 marks)

Remember that the actual exam paper will offer you a choice of two of these 33-mark questions. As this is a sample question, here there is only one. In the exam, you should read each question carefully before you decide which one to answer, making sure that you have sufficient knowledge to write a good analytical and evaluative answer with relevant examples.

(e) This question asks you to 'assess' a particular view about the functions of religion. In order to do this, you will need to show that you have a clear understanding of the view, such as who holds it, and what they offer as arguments and evidence. You should then look at an alternative view (or views), together with the arguments and evidence offered, and assess the strengths and weaknesses of the different viewpoints.

Total: 60 marks

A-grade student

(01) One problem is that the statistics may be inaccurate **a**. For example, if they relate to a morning service, they may miss those who go to worship in the evening, but if they include both times of day, there may be a risk of double counting, as some people may go to church more than once in the day **b**.

A second problem is that they assume that only those who go to church have a religious belief **a**. Many people may choose to worship at home, and some may worship at informal religious gatherings that would be missed by the statistics. As Item A says, there has been a significant opening up of religious identities outside of the traditional religious institutions **b c**.

A third problem is that there is an assumed relationship between church attendance and belief **a**. Particularly in the case of the Church of England, many people see going to church as a social, rather than a religious, obligation, and may attend as a formality without having a true belief **b**. It is often said that the Church of England is the Tory party at prayer, indicating that people see it as 'the done thing' to go to church to keep up a certain status in society **d**.

(e) This is a very good answer. The three parts are clearly separated, and for each one, **a** the first sentence identifies the problem, **b** while the remainder clearly explains it. **c** There is a useful reference to the Item, although this was not specifically asked for. The third part of the answer is unnecessarily long. **b** The second sentence gives sufficient explanation, and **d** there was no need to include additional material.

(e) **9/9 marks**

(02) As Item A points out, although more than half of young people questioned say that they are not religious, some young people see religion as very important in their lives **a**. The 2005 Church Census showed that only about 5% of young people aged 15–19 were regular churchgoers **b**. One thing to point out is that the information in Item A comes from studies such as the British Social Attitudes Survey. It is possible that some young people, who actually do have religious feelings, when questioned said that they were not religious, as they were embarrassed to admit their religiosity, thinking that it was not 'cool' **c**. However, the general trend in British society is for people to be less religious, so we can probably assume that many young people do not have deeply-felt religious beliefs **d**.

(e) This is a very good opening paragraph. **a** It refers directly to Item A, as required by the question, and does more than simply paraphrase or quote directly. **b** Good knowledge and understanding are shown by giving an example which supports the information in Item A, thus fulfilling the 'and elsewhere' part of the question. **c** The student also uses Item A to point out a possible flaw in the survey method, namely, that people may not always give truthful answers. **d** Having pointed out a possible flaw, the student then shows evaluation by linking the statement about the loss of religiosity among young people to a more general trend in society.

> Though not much research has been carried out into young people and religious belief **e**, in 2005 David Voas published some research on this issue. He found that, where there were two religious parents in a family, they had a 50:50 chance of passing on their religious beliefs to their children. Where there was only one religious parent, there was only a one-in-four chance of the children being religious, while where neither parent was religious, the children were also likely to have no religious belief **f**. This suggests that those young people who are religious probably come from 'religious' families. Again, as the number of religious adults declines, it is likely that there will be fewer religious young people, unless they become religious converts when they are older **g**.

(e) **e** This paragraph continues to focus on the question of children/young people and religious devotion, **f** quoting some relevant research and **g** then going on to show good knowledge, understanding and analysis.

> There is, however, another reason why some young people may show 'an increasing intensity of religious devotion', and it highlights the problems of thinking only about Christianity **h**. For many young people from ethnic minority families, living in Britain is not easy, and they may feel marginalised and excluded from mainstream society. For many of these young people, religion becomes an important part of their identity, and provides them with a sense of community and belonging. This seems to be the case with many young Muslims. Research by Mirza et al. (2007) **i** showed that religious identity and values were increasingly important to second and third generation young Muslims **j**. Whereas their parents tended to try to 'blend in' and adapt to the British way of life, younger Muslims are increasingly prepared to express their religious identity publicly. For example, many young Muslim girls and women choose to wear the hijab, even though their mothers do not do so. Mirza et al. also argue that many of the measures designed to protect Muslims and acknowledge their different religious beliefs, such as anti-racist laws, faith schools etc. serve to reinforce the idea that Muslims are 'different', and can emphasise the importance of a separate religious identity.
>
> Other young people in groups at risk of being marginalised, such as Afro-Caribbeans, may also show increasing religious devotion, especially where they are brought up in Pentecostal or other evangelical Christian families **j**. Again, as with the early sects, religious belief and membership of a religious community can act as a buffer and compensate for social exclusion, poverty and deprivation **k**.

(e) **h** These two paragraphs remain tightly focused on the set question, and show a sound knowledge and understanding of the issues, for example, the problems of focusing on Christianity. **i** There is good and accurate knowledge of relevant research, and **j** reference is made to two different religious faiths, **k** with a nice link made between current evangelical Christianity and early Christian sects.

In conclusion, there are a number of reasons why some young people may show increased religious devotion. While in some cases it is because of family upbringing, in others it reflects social exclusion and the decline of other forms of social identity, such as work, neighbourhood and social class.

ⓔ The student attempts here to draw the arguments together to form a conclusion. This kind of conclusion, which is in effect a brief summary of the arguments and evidence presented in the main part of the answer, can be very effective, as is the case here. Remember that, with an 18-mark question such as this, only 20–25 minutes should be spent on the answer, so it is not expected that students will be able to present all the arguments and evidence at their disposal. This student has done as much as can be reasonably expected in the time available and has stuck closely to the set question.

ⓔ AO1: 6/6 + AO2: 11/12 = 17/18 marks

(03) The view that social institutions continue to exist because they perform important functions for society is, of course, a functionalist view **a**. Durkheim **b**, a major functionalist and one of the founding fathers of sociology, believed that one of religion's main functions was to bring the people of a society together, and to reinforce social norms and values **c**. However, much of Durkheim's ideas about this were formed from the study of simple, small-scale societies or even tribes, so it is arguable whether this view can be applied to large-scale societies, particularly modern or postmodern ones, with their complex structure and multitude of different religious faiths **d**. Bellah, a neo-functionalist, also believes that religion still performs essential functions. He says that a process of individuation has occurred, leaving people to look for religious meaning through individual experience, rather than through an organisation such as an established church **e**.

ⓔ A good opening paragraph, which immediately locates the view expressed in the question to a particular **a** social theory and **b** a sociologist. **c** Having briefly explained what Durkheim regarded as one of religion's major functions, **d** the student shows evaluation by pointing out a possible problem with the view. **e** Good knowledge and understanding is also shown by referring to the views of a neo-functionalist.

Another classical sociologist, Karl Marx, thought that religious beliefs were based on superstition, and that the traditional forms of religion would disappear once rational, scientific knowledge became more widespread in society. Marx believed that religion served to bring comfort to the oppressed working class, and it could be argued that enforced changes in the way that capitalists treated their workers, together with the development of the welfare state, would lessen the need for religious beliefs as a source of comfort **f**.

ⓔ **f** The student here shows further knowledge and understanding of sociological theory, presenting a contrasting view to that of Durkheim. Note that the student has yet to address the set question directly. This is still fine at this point, but remember that it is important to keep an eye on the time, and to make sure that you do not spend too long before getting down to the 'meat' of your answer.

It is obvious, not only from Britain but from many other countries that, even though there is evidence of growing secularisation, religion is still important to many people on a personal level, and that religious institutions still have some power. Is this linked to the functions it performs, and if it is, what are those functions?

Despite the changes in society and a possible move towards more meritocracy, it is true that some people are still marginalised and oppressed. For them, religious beliefs can bring hope of a better life in the next world, and comfort and support to help with the pain of this world **g**. It could be argued that having this comfort prevents such people from becoming more radical and demanding change. For those in power, this could be seen as an important function for society, as it serves to prevent radical change and possible social upheaval **h**.

e The student now moves to addressing the set question directly, and **g** gives one example of a possibly important function performed by religion. It would be helpful to give an example of a marginalised or oppressed group for whom religion could provide comfort. **h** Note that analysis and evaluation are shown by suggesting that only some people ('those in power') might see the possible prevention of radicalisation as functionally important.

In some countries, such as Britain, there is a divide between religious institutions and the state, although the Church of England has a role to play in certain state functions (the coronation of the monarch) and some of its bishops sit in the House of Lords. Some people argue, though, that religious organisations such as the Church of England are important because they can provide a check to the power of the state **i**. Leading church leaders, such as the Archbishop of Canterbury, have spoken out against social issues such as poverty, and some of those who take part in protests — for example against the war in Iraq — have strong religious views **j**. Again, the British state has made some concessions to religious beliefs, for example, allowing animals to be slaughtered according to Jewish and Islamic laws.

In the USA **k**, religious leaders such as Martin Luther King were important figures in the Civil Rights movement, and the efforts of these leaders and their followers helped to force the US state to end segregation and discrimination against black Americans.

e An interesting couple of paragraphs, looking at **i** how religion can sometimes act as a buffer against the power of the state and **j** provide a means of social protest. **k** Note that the student provides a relevant example from another society, which shows breadth of knowledge.

Another important function of religion in modern Britain (as it was in the past) is to provide various welfare functions, often seen today as 'plugging the gaps' in the welfare state. For example, the Salvation Army provides funds and shelter for individuals and families in need, and also runs a service giving information about runaway children to let their family know that they are alright. Other religious organisations provide help and support for drug and alcohol addicts and people with AIDS and even run adoption agencies. Many religious groups also raise money for aid to poor countries **l**.

e **l** The student provides further relevant examples of some important functions performed by religious groups.

However, there are also arguments that religion is sometimes dysfunctional for society, or at least some parts of it. The 'right to life' movement, in the UK but especially in the USA, has caused not just distress but also actual harm to women seeking an abortion and doctors involved in providing abortions **m**. The teachings of the Roman Catholic Church against contraception and divorce can also be seen as dysfunctional for some families, even though many followers do not obey the Pope, especially where contraception is concerned **n**. The radicalisation of some young Muslims, leading to terror attacks in Britain and the USA, is another example of where religion can be dysfunctional **o**. Again, the Taliban in Afghanistan have proved very dysfunctional to females, stopping girls from going to school and not letting women work outside the home or have similar freedoms to men **p**. It can, therefore, be argued that not all the roles played by religion in society are good.

e **m, n, o, p** Evaluation is shown here by offering some well chosen examples of where religion can be seen as dysfunctional. Note that the student recognises that certain groups may be more affected than others by these aspects of religion.

In conclusion, it can be seen that, even in so-called secular societies, religion can perform important functions. However, some aspects of religion can also be dysfunctional, both for groups of individuals and for society.

e A brief but adequate conclusion reminding the examiner that the student has discussed both positive and negative aspects of the functions performed by religion and religious organisations.

e **AO1: 15/15 + AO2 (a): 7/9 + AO2 (b): 9/9 = 31/33 marks**

e **Overall: 57/60 marks**

C-grade student

(01) ● Lots of people believe in things such as New Age spiritualism, which means that they have faith but don't go to church.

● Not all religions are included.

● Some people get counted twice.

e While the student is correct in thinking that these short-answer questions may be answered with a series of bullet points, it is important to provide enough information to gain the marks.

The first point identifies a reason (belief in New Age spiritualism) and gives a brief explanation of how this is linked to (non) church attendance. This is just enough to score 3 marks. The second point gives a reason why attendance statistics might be unreliable, but no explanation, so gains only 1 mark. The third point again gives an acceptable reason, but fails to explain how and why some people might be counted twice, so gains only 1 of the 3 available marks.

ℯ 5/9 marks

> **(02)** As Item A says, there is an increasing intensity of religious devotion among a minority of young people **a**. In some cases this could be due to peer pressure, such as the 'Silver Ring Thing' among some US girls, where they wear a ring as a promise not to have sex before they are married **b**.

ℯ a Although the student makes an immediate reference to Item A, it is just to repeat a phrase; there is no discussion or development. While reference to Item A is important, the material should be used in some way to present or develop an argument. At this point, it looks as though the student has already moved on, though further appropriate reference may be made later. **b** A potentially relevant example is offered, but the student does not draw out how wearing the silver ring is linked to religious devotion. The examiners are all sociologists, but even so, you should try to make sure that they can see that you understand the significance of what you are writing in terms of the set question.

> As Britain is now a mainly secular society, with religion losing social significance **c**, it seems strange that some young people are becoming more religious. However, it is mainly the established Christian churches that are declining, and many young people will have been brought up in other faiths, e.g. Islam or Sikhism **d**. These are usually more religious than Christianity **e**, so some of the young people could come from these backgrounds.

ℯ c There is some evidence that the student understands what is meant by 'secular', and **d** a good point is made about the decline in established Christian churches rather than across all faiths and types of religious organisation. However, it is not clear exactly what is meant by **e** the statement that faiths such as Islam or Sikhism are 'more religious' than Christianity. Again, the student is not spelling out clearly the line of argument. Even answers to shorter essay questions should show a clear line of argument, with supporting points and evidence.

> Some immigrants to Britain, even from Christian countries such as Poland, are more religious than native British people, and many of these immigrants are younger, so this could also be an explanation of why some young people are religious **f**. Some people from ethnic minority groups might want to express their solidarity with Muslims from other countries as a result of the 'war on terror' and the war in Iraq. This could mean that they felt stronger links to their religion and it became more important to them **g**.

ℯ f A good link is made between the age of some immigrants and the greater religiosity of their country of origin. **g** The point about religious identity and the 'war on terror' is potentially a very good one, though unfortunately the student does not show how this might be linked to age.

Item A doesn't say what people meant by 'religious' **h**, so some answers could have been referring to non-traditional religious beliefs and practices such as New Ageism or spiritualism **i**.

e **h** Another reference to Item A, this time using the information rather than simply repeating it, and an evaluative point referring to the lack of information about whether or not there was a shared definition of 'religious' in the studies/surveys, which is potentially an important issue. **i** However, the point about non-traditional beliefs and practices should be developed — why might young people be attracted to such beliefs? The answer ends very abruptly, without any attempt at a conclusion. There are several missed opportunities here, resulting in lost marks for this student.

e **AO1: 3/6 + AO2: 8/12 = 11/18 marks**

---

(03) Although Britain is now considered to be a secular society, religion still seems to be important. Though church attendance is falling, some people still attend church regularly, and some churches are even growing. In surveys about religious belief, most people say that they have some kind of belief or faith, though sometimes this is in a 'spirit' or 'life force' rather than God **a**.

Examiner tip
It is always a good idea to make a clear reference to the set question (without simply repeating it) as soon as possible in your answer. This should help to keep you on the right track.

e **a** The knowledge presented here is accurate and potentially relevant to the question. However, the student has not yet picked up on the idea of the 'functions' of religion, and whether or not these are important.

Many sociologists thought that, as scientific ideas became more widespread, the need for religious explanations of the world would disappear, or at least decrease, but this doesn't really seem to be the case **b**. Richard Dawkins is attacked by many people for his views on religion and his atheistic beliefs, and even David Attenborough has said that he receives hate mail from people because he doesn't acknowledge or praise God in his programmes about the wonders of wildlife. The argument about teaching creationism in schools highlights the fact that some people still prefer religious beliefs to scientific ones **c**.

Examiner tip
It is really important to make sure that your answer addresses the set question, and this is where a brief essay plan can help.

e The student now seems in danger of ignoring the issues raised by the question, and seems to be offering an answer on secularisation. **b** The first sentence could have been linked to the functions of religion, i.e. religion offers an explanation of important questions about the world, but does not do so. **c** Note that the information here is largely general, without a clear sociological focus.

Again, while the power of the church is much less than it was in medieval times, it still has power. Church of England bishops sit in the House of Lords, and Roman Catholics the world over accept the power of the Pope to tell them how they should live their lives **d**. If we look at other religions, Islam in particular is a powerful force in society, and has shown (e.g. in Iran) how religious ideas can bring about social change, such as the overthrow of the shah. Marxists argue that, under some circumstances, religion can bring about social change rather than always supporting the status quo e.

Ⓔ d There is still no focus on the set question, and the student is likely to lose many valuable marks by not using arguments and evidence clearly relevant to the question asked. Can you think of ways in which at least some of the information presented could be made relevant to the set question? e There is a reference to social theory in the last sentence, but this, too, is not linked to the question.

So why is religion still important for society f? For some people it brings comfort — for example, people who are poor or oppressed. For some immigrants it reminds them of home, such as the many Polish people who are practising Roman Catholics. Some Muslims see their religious beliefs as an important part of their identity, as their religion covers all aspects of their lives g. Functionalists argue that social institutions only last if they are important for society, although some can become dysfunctional over time h.

Ⓔ f The student at last begins to focus on the reasons for the importance of religion, although the reference to 'functions' is still implicit. g The examples presented focus on the importance to individuals, rather than to society. This is legitimate, although some link should be provided regarding why importance to individuals might also be important to society. h The last sentence is, of course, relevant, and in a good answer would be developed further. Here it appears to be added almost as a last-minute afterthought.

Again, religion can act to bring people together. There are often religious ceremonies and services after disasters or personal tragedies, such as the remembrance service for Princess Diana, and the church services after the 11 September bombings in the USA, the tsunami and the Australian bush fires. It is thought that taking part in acts of collective worship helps people to cope with their grief, and also acts as a mark of respect. It could also help people to think of the disaster as an act of God, rather than the fault of a person, company or government i.

Ⓔ Here there is an attempt to look at the possible functions of religion for society. i The line of argument is still presented largely through examples.

> **Examiner tip**
> While examples are a good way of showing appropriate knowledge and understanding, they should always be linked to clear sociological arguments.

Even if religion has lost its functions as far as the whole society is concerned, it can be functional for some minority groups j. It can give them comfort and moral support if they are suffering from social exclusion, and taking part in collective acts of worship with others of their group can help to keep their culture alive and also help them to make friends k.

Ⓔ j An important point is being made here, namely that religion might offer different functions for different groups. k The example given is appropriate and clearly linked to the discussion of functions for minority groups.

Durkheim, a functionalist, believed that religion was important because one function was that its beliefs and practices helped to bind people into a shared community. Durkheim based these ideas on his study of a simple Aboriginal society, and it is clear that in today's Western multicultural societies not only are religious beliefs and practices different for different groups, but it is more difficult to talk of a single community with shared beliefs. In fact, some religious beliefs, such as women wearing the full veil, can bring people into conflict with the laws of the state, as is the case now in France **l**. Malinowski, another functionalist, said that religion helped people to make sense of the world in times of uncertainty, and gave them a sense of security and belonging. This was shown by the upsurge in religious feelings and worship after the 9/11 attacks in the USA **m**.

ⓔ At last there is an attempt to discuss sociological beliefs about the functions of religion. After a very brief mention of one of Durkheim's ideas, there are some evaluative comments regarding the problems of applying this to modern Western societies, and **l** an appropriate example is used to illustrate this. It is a pity that this occurs so late in the answer. **m** However, the student goes on to identify another functionalist, and again provides an example to illustrate the point made.

Finally, it is getting more and more difficult to talk about religion. As well as the major world religions, there has been a growth in 'pick'n'mix' religion, with people turning to various types of New Age beliefs, and some people joining cults and sects. For some people, this kind of belief can help them to express themselves as individuals, or find support and comfort being in a group of people with shared beliefs **n**. So, although Britain is in one sense mainly a secular society, religion still performs important functions **o**.

ⓔ This paragraph raises a potentially very important point, namely what exactly do we mean by religion? **n** If you can raise this issue earlier, it will give you the opportunity to engage in a sociological debate, while still focusing on the issue of 'functions'. Overall, this is a weak conclusion. **o** The student has missed the opportunity to present the sociological arguments and so has been unable to present a stronger and more relevant conclusion.

ⓔ AO1: 10/15 + AO2 (a): 5/9 + AO2 (b): 4/9 = 19/33 marks

ⓔ Overall: 35/60 marks

Example 2 Defining religion; sects; religion and social change

Read Item A below and answer questions 01 and 02 that follow. Then answer question 03.

Item A

There have been many attempts to arrive at a clear definition of a sect. Weber's ideal type defined the sect largely in terms of how it differed from a church. For example, membership of a sect is usually by conversion, whereas many people are born into a particular church, and do not have to prove anything to become a member. Some sects arise when a group breaks away from an established religious organisation, often as a result of a disagreement over doctrine. Wallis defined a sect in terms of its relationship to the world, i.e. whether it was 'world-affirming' or 'world-rejecting'. Many sects emphasise their exclusiveness — only those who show themselves to be worthy are accepted as members. It is suggested that membership of sects increases in times of rapid social change, when both personal anxiety and social disorganisation may be high. It is important to remember that sects can arise from religions other than Christianity, for example the Falun Gong of China and the Aum Shinrikyo of Japan.

(01) Identify and briefly explain three problems of defining what is meant by 'religion'.   (9 marks)

ⓔ It is often useful with this type of question to jot down first what you think the three problems are, and then write out each one together with its brief explanation. Remember to show clearly that there are three separate points. You should spend about 10 minutes on this type of question, so make sure that you do not write explanations that are too long and detailed.

(02) Using material from Item A and elsewhere, examine the problems of measuring the extent of sect membership in society.   (18 marks)

ⓔ You should only spend about 20 minutes on this question, so you may not be able to examine all the possible problems raised by it. It is usually better to select some that you consider to be particularly important and write something about each, than to make a long list that does not explain or discuss anything properly. In this example, you should think about the different types of sect and their relationship to the wider society — are some more problematic than others in terms of measuring membership, and if so, why? Think also about the length of time that a sect has been in existence. Are there additional problems in defining what we mean by a sect? Are there methodological problems in measuring sect membership?

(03) 'Far from always being a conservative force in society, religious beliefs can act to promote social change.' To what extent is this view supported by sociological arguments and evidence?   (33 marks)

(e) Make sure that your answer contains both sociological arguments (which sociologists believe what) and evidence (what we examine to try to determine who has the stronger case). A good start would be to identify and briefly discuss which sociologist(s) or theoretical perspective(s) would argue that religious beliefs always (note the possible significance of this word) act as a conservative force in society — be sure to make it clear that you know what 'a conservative force' means in this context. You could then discuss who might argue, or has argued, that religious beliefs can promote social change (note the importance of the use of 'promote' rather than 'cause'). That would take care of your sociological arguments, and then you would need to discuss what evidence there is on each side. Your conclusion, which need not necessarily come down firmly on one side or the other, should draw together briefly the case that you have made in your essay.

Total: 60 marks

A-grade student

(01) • One problem is whether to use an 'inclusivist' definition, which accepts belief systems without reference to a god or supernatural being, or to use 'exclusivist' definitions, which say that there has to be some reference to a supernatural being or beings with powers to affect life on earth. Different definitions lead to different things being classified as 'religion'.

• We need to know what counts as 'religious'. Do we mean people who just say that they have a religious belief, or only people who show some kind of religious commitment, e.g. praying or going to services?

• We also need to consider size. Do we count only 'world religions' with mass membership, or do we also include the beliefs of very small groups? This can have implications for studying secularisation.

(e) Three good reasons, each with a clear explanation.

(e) **9/9 marks**

(02) As Item A suggests, there are different ways of defining exactly what a sect is **a**. Sometimes, particularly in the mass media, the terms 'sect' and 'cult' are used as if they were the same thing, though there are differences between them, one being that the cult is usually less structured and organised than the sect. If sociologists do not have a shared definition of what we mean by a sect **b**, there is an obvious problem in defining how many people are sect members.

(e) A good start — **a** it makes immediate and relevant reference to Item A and **b** goes on to identify an important difficulty of measuring the extent of sect membership.

Sometimes a sect arises as a breakaway movement from a church, often because some people disagree with the teachings or leadership **c**. Examples of this would be the Baptists and Congregationalists **d**. However, we now regard these groups as denominations, so another problem is the point in time at which the sect is measured. If one difference between a sect and a denomination is the level of organisation, how much organisation does there have to be before we decide that something is a denomination and not a sect **e**?

(e) This is a good paragraph. Note how the student first gives **c** a way in which a sect might arise, then gives some **d** examples of where this has happened, and then **e** links this to the problem outlined in the question.

> Another problem is that, as Item A points out, some sects are 'world-rejecting' (Wallis) **f**. This means that they avoid contact with the wider society, and are often very secretive **g**. It would be difficult in these cases for a sociologist to find out how many people were members, as members of these sects tend to live in closed communities **h**. Eileen Barker is one of the few sociologists to do in-depth research into a sect, with her work *The Making of a Moonie* **i**.

(e) **f** Another relevant reference to Item A— **g** which is then explained— **h** linked to the problem raised by the question and **i** finished off with an appropriate example.

> If a sect is world-affirming, it still could be difficult to measure the extent of membership as some of these sects (e.g. the TM movement) are very secretive and have a 'shifting' membership, in that people seem to move in and out **j**, so it would depend on the point at which membership was measured **k**.

(e) **j** Another appropriate difficulty identified and explained. **k** This student clearly understands the methodological problem of the importance of the particular point in time at which something is measured.

> It is hard to see how sociologists could easily measure sect membership just by asking people about their religious beliefs and practices. Apart from the sheer size of such a survey (sect membership is quite low, so you would have to ask a lot of people to find some sect members), many people would not give you that information anyway, especially if the sect was one that was engaged in activities that were criminal (e.g. the Japanese Supreme Truth) or suicidal (e.g. Heaven's Gate) **l**. This means that, in some cases, the only way would be for a participant observation study, which, with some sects, would have to be covert **m**. This would be very time consuming, and could be dangerous, if the sect was engaged in criminal activities.

(e) **l** A further example of the problems of measuring sect membership, supported by some appropriate examples and also **m** showing knowledge of methodological issues.

> In conclusion, it is very difficult to measure the extent of sect membership in society.

(e) This is a weak conclusion, which neither summarises the discussion nor adds anything to it. However, overall this is a good answer, showing the need for a tight focus in this type of 18-mark question.

(e) **AO1: 6/6 + AO2: 10/12 = 16/18 marks**

(03) The idea that religion acts as a conservative force in society is associated with the functionalists **a**. Durkheim **b** believed that, through shared rituals and beliefs, religion created social solidarity, and the passing on of these beliefs and rituals helped to maintain the status quo. However, Marx **b** also saw religion mainly as a conservative force, as he believed that it had an ideological role, namely supporting capitalism and helping to maintain the power of the capitalists.

ⓔ This is a good opening paragraph. **a** The view expressed in the statement is correctly identified as a functionalist view. **b** There is accurate reference to the views of two classical sociologists and the reference to Marx is used to show that he too saw religion as a conservative force.

The idea that religion can promote social change is usually associated with Max Weber **c**. In his 'Protestant ethic' thesis, Weber tried to show that, under certain conditions, religious beliefs could make people act in such a way that social change took place. Weber's example was of the Calvinists, whose beliefs led them to work hard in their 'calling' but not to spend their money on worldly goods and luxuries. In this way, they amassed a great deal of capital which they could invest in the new technologies and working practices that underpinned the Industrial Revolution **d**.

ⓔ The student now moves on to discuss the ideas of religion and social change, again using a **c** classical sociologist to show good knowledge and understanding of social theory. **d** Note how the temptation to give a lengthy description of Weber's work has been avoided.

However, Gramsci — a neo-Marxist — showed how the ideas of religion could be interpreted in a way that was different from what the capitalists intended; for example, believing that religion said that it was a duty to help the poor and oppressed. This leads to the idea of liberation theology, a movement in 1960s and 1970s Latin America, in which religious leaders — mainly Catholic priests — helped to fight poverty and injustice in the name of religion. Gramsci said that no group could achieve total hegemony, so there was always some room for different interpretations **e**.

ⓔ **e** This is evaluation of the classical Marxist idea by juxtaposition, meaning that the student has used another perspective (neo-Marxism) to show how Marxist ideas can be used in a different way.

The views of religious fundamentalists, such as the New Christian Right in the USA, can also be used to bring about social change. The NCR forms a strong political force and has successfully managed in some states to bring about changes in the law — for example with regard to abortion and gay marriage — where it has managed to overturn or prevent more liberal policies on these issues. It is still fighting these and other matters, such as the teaching of creationism rather than evolution in schools **f**.

ⓔ **f** Though brief, this paragraph provides interesting examples of the influence of certain religious ideas.

> If we look at other religions, not just at Christianity, we can also see that sometimes religious ideas are linked to social change. A good example would be the revolution in Iran **g**, in which the shah was overthrown and the ayatollahs, or religious leaders, took control. There are other examples of religious fundamentalism where people's beliefs and practices have brought about social change. We could think of the many ways that Western society has changed, with the so-called 'war on terror' following the 11 September attacks in the USA **g** and the 7 July attacks in London **g**. Again, the very strict interpretation of Islamic law by the Taliban in Afghanistan **g** has led to changes in that society, many of them with negative effects on women and girls, who have far less freedom than they did before.

ⓔ **g** This is a very good paragraph, showing wide-ranging knowledge and understanding of religious ideas other than Christian ones that are linked to social change.

> In conclusion, while many religious ideas and practices have been, and still are, linked to maintaining the status quo, there are many examples in society where they are also linked to bringing about social change.

ⓔ This is a brief but adequate conclusion, in which the student reminds the reader of the preceding arguments and evidence.

ⓔ **AO1: 12/15 + AO2 (a): 8/9 + AO2 (b): 8/9 = 28/33 marks**

ⓔ **Overall: 53/60 marks**

C-grade student

(01) • Deciding whether there has to be a belief in a god or being with supernatural powers, or just a belief in some kind of 'life force' with no special power to influence worldly affairs.

• How you define religion affects the results.

• Whether to look at the formal structures of religion, e.g. established churches, or at the effects on individuals (religious behaviour), or both. People might have a religious faith but not belong to any church.

ⓔ The first point made is an acceptable problem, with an adequate explanation. However, the second point is not clear (what results?) and is rather a consequence of the problems of definition, rather than a problem of definition in its own right. The third point is acceptable, as is the brief explanation.

ⓔ **6/9 marks**

(02) As Item A says, there have been many attempts to arrive at a clear definition of a sect **a**. Some sects have made headlines around the world — for example the members of the Branch Davidians at Waco and the mass suicide of the members of the People's Temple at Jonestown and the Heaven's Gate members **b**. People might not have even heard of these sects if people hadn't died because of them.

💬 **a** This student has clearly been instructed about the importance of making reference to Item A. However, all that happens here is that the first sentence is reproduced and then the student goes on to talk about something entirely different. To gain higher marks, the student would need to make the point that attempts to measure sect membership will be affected by the definition (of a sect) that is used. There are, however, **b** three examples of sects given and the implicit suggestion that there has to be knowledge of the existence of a sect before there can be any attempt to gauge its membership.

It is easier to measure sect membership if the sect is world affirming, because there won't be a need for secrecy — the sect might even advertise for members, or publish membership lists. A lot of world rejecting sects are very secretive, and cut themselves off from the world, so it would be hard for a sociologist to know about these **c**, except through covert participant observation, which could be difficult and dangerous **d**.

💬 The use of the terms 'world affirming' and 'world rejecting' is implicit reference to Item A, and **c** the student gives acceptable reasons why it might be easier to measure membership of the first scenario than the second. **d** No reasons are given regarding why covert participant observation might be 'difficult and dangerous', though there is clearly understanding of the method and the circumstances under which it might be used. Remember that it is important, where relevant, to make reference to sociological theories and methods.

Item A says that membership of sects increases in times of rapid social change. This could be another problem of measurement **e**. If there is a lot of social change, then people could join a sect but just for a short while, and then move out or move away or join a different one. So you could get different numbers depending on when you did the counting **e**.

💬 **e** Here the student's reference to Item A is followed by a clear link to the question.

Another problem of measurement could be when looking at sects in other societies, such as the ones mentioned in Item A **f**. There would be difficulties for Western sociologists to get knowledge of these sects unless they spoke the language, and also the sect could be engaged in illegal activities, like the gas attack on the Japanese underground **g**.

💬 **f** Further difficulties of measuring sect membership are given, again using Item A, and **g** knowledge is shown of the activities of the Aum Shinrikyo sect, though the reference is not made explicit. There are other problems of measurement, which are not mentioned here, but in a shorter-mark question it is not usually necessary or possible to include all points. The student shows reasonable knowledge and understanding here, though analysis and evaluation are relatively weak.

> Last, as Item A says, there is no clear definition of what we mean by a sect **h**. Different sociologists could have different ideas, which would affect the outcome. It also takes a long time to do research, so by the time it was finished, it could already be out of date **i**.

(e) **h** The student finally picks up on this important point raised by Item A, **i** and also offers a further problem of measuring the extent of sect membership. There is no attempt to write a conclusion.

(e) **AO1: 4/6 + AO2: 7/12 = 11/18 marks**

> **(03)** Marx said that religion was ideological **a**, that it made the workers believe that everything was according to God's plan, so that it justified the power of the capitalists. Religious ideas served two purposes, to keep the existing social order and to give the oppressed working class comfort, as they were promised that life would be better in the next world **b**.

(e) **a** The student has jumped straight in here. Marxist ideas on religion are presented, **b** though the link to these and religion being a conservative force in society is largely implicit.

> Weber said that religion caused social change. He believed that the ideas of the Protestant work ethic brought about capitalism and the Industrial Revolution, which was a huge social change **c**. Countries without the Protestant work ethic took much longer to industrialise.

(e) The summary of Weber's thesis is not quite accurate, **c** but the notion of the link between the Protestant work ethic and social change is evident.

> Religion can also be a conservative force when it won't allow for new ideas. This happened when Galileo tried to show that the earth moved round the sun, and not the other way round, which was the teaching of the church. He was tried for heresy and spent the last years of his life under house arrest. Religious conservatism is also shown in the fact that the Christian religion did not want to accept women priests (Roman Catholics still don't) or allow divorced couples to marry in church **d**.

(e) **d** Further examples of religion acting as a conservative force are given. However, the main thrust of the question concerns religion and social change, so the student needs to begin to address this aspect of the question in more detail.

> Liberation theology shows that religion can promote social change. Priests in South America worked hard to improve the lot of the oppressed workers, saying

that Jesus taught that you should help the poor in society. Fundamentalists also want social change. In their case, they want to 'turn back the clock' and return to what they consider to be the original beliefs and practices of their religion. To do this, they want to get rid of what they see as the immoral practices seen in modern society and 'get back to basics'. In some cases they have succeeded, e.g. the Iranian revolution e.

The US president, Barack Obama, is a religious man who believes that it is his duty to improve the condition of the black US population, who were among his strongest supporters. However, George W. Bush was also religious (a born-again Christian) and he was right-wing and did little to help the poor of the USA f, so we see that religion can be a conservative force and a force for social change g.

(e) e Some relevant examples of religious ideas linked to social change, f and an interesting example of the religious beliefs of two US presidents. There is no conclusion as such, g though the last part of the final sentence attempts to bring the two parts of the question together.

Functionalists like Durkheim h also believe that religion is conservative. He believed that when people worshipped their god (or totem pole), they were in fact worshipping their own society. Durkheim said that coming together in acts of worship reminded people of what were the shared norms and values of their society. This made it harder for people to go against those norms, and so helped to keep the society stable and unchanging. Durkheim has been criticised, though, for looking at very small simple societies, and some sociologists say that his ideas aren't relevant to today's society.

(e) It looks very much as though this paragraph is an afterthought, and shows the need for even a brief plan before starting on an essay. Nevertheless, the material is broadly accurate and relevant to the question, in that h it presents another sociological view on religion acting as a conservative force in society

(e) **AO1: 9/15 + AO2 (a): 6/9 + AO2 (b): 5/9 = 20/33 marks**

(e) **Overall: 37/60 marks**

Example 3 Church attendance and age; church attendance and ethnicity; religious fundamentalism

Read Item A below and answer questions 01 and 02 that follow. Then answer question 03.

Item A

The major findings from the 2005 Church Census, undertaken by Christian Research, show that many churches in England are in a healthier state now than 7 years ago. Some local churches, as well as a few denominations, are doing very well, more churches are growing, and overall they are not losing nearly as many people as they were. The Census showed that in the 1990s, 1 million people left church in 9 years, but in the 7 years from 1998 to 2005, only half a million left, a much slower rate of decline. There are two major reasons for this slowing decline: the number of churches which are growing, and a considerable increase of ethnic minority churchgoers, especially black people. However, the declining churches are still losing more people than the growing churches are gaining. The net effect is that overall, 6.3% of the population are now in church on an average Sunday, down from 7.5% in 1998. A major factor in this decline is that churchgoers are significantly older on average than the population — 29% of churchgoers are 65 or over, compared with 16% of the population.

Source: adapted from P. Brierley (2006) *Pulling out of the Nosedive*, Christian Research.

(01) Identify and briefly explain three reasons why older people may attend church more frequently than younger people. (9 marks)

Ⓕ Make sure that you keep the focus here on age, rather than other social divisions.

(02) Using material from Item A and elsewhere, examine some of the reasons for the increase in churchgoers from ethnic minority backgrounds. (18 marks)

ⓔ You should think of some of the sociological suggestions that have been put forward regarding the role and function of religion in people's lives. Is there a function that might apply particularly to people from ethnic minority groups? If so, why? Are there any social factors that could be involved? Although the Item is referring to 'church', you might broaden this out to include other places of worship, but make sure you keep focused on the question asked.

(03) Assess the view that the rise of religious fundamentalism will inevitably lead to social conflict. (33 marks)

ⓔ You should show as early as possible in your answer that you understand what is meant by 'religious fundamentalism'. You could then discuss why it might be thought that this would lead to social conflict. Note the word 'inevitably' — questioning this could give you important marks for evaluation. In order to assess the view expressed, you will need to provide a range of examples, preferably showing where fundamentalist views have, and have not, led to social conflict. There is an opportunity here to use a wide range of examples, drawn from different societies and religions.

Total: 60 marks

A-grade student

(01) Older people grew up in a time when it was more normal to go to church on Sundays, so they are more likely to have continued the habit. Their childhood socialisation has taught them to do this.

Older people will be retired, so will have more time to go to church, whereas people of working age might have to use Sundays (or other worship days) to do other things, e.g. housework or shopping.

Research has shown that women tend to be more 'religious' than men, and as women have a longer life expectancy than men they are more likely to be at church.

(e) The first two reasons are acceptable, and each has a suitable explanation. However, although the statement given in the third point is accurate, it is not actually a reason why older people may attend church more frequently than younger people so cannot be awarded any marks.

(e) **6/9 marks**

---

(02) Item A points out that the considerable increase in the number of ethnic minority churchgoers has helped to slow the decline in churchgoing in the UK **a**. The Item doesn't make clear whether the Church Census referred to church membership or church attendance, and presumably is referring only to Christian churches **b**. However, we need to examine the reasons for this.

(e) This is a good opening paragraph. **a** While the student clearly and accurately uses material from Item A, the material is paraphrased, and not simply repeated word for word. **b** Questioning the Item itself by pointing out a lack of clarity demonstrates good evaluation. The final sentence suggests that the student is immediately going to address the set question.

One reason can be linked to Weber's idea of the 'theodicy of disprivilege' **c**. Weber said that certain religious groups, mainly sects, appealed to the poorer and downtrodden members of society as they explained deprivation as God's way of testing faith, and promised that rewards for suffering would be given in heaven. This is also linked to Marx' view of religion as 'the opium of the people' **c**, that is, something which deadened the pain of their everyday lives. As many members of ethnic minority groups are among the least privileged in our society, and often suffer from poverty and abuse, this would explain why such people might be more likely to be churchgoers than other, more affluent, groups **d**. These ideas are particularly found in evangelical churches, and these have a high proportion of people from ethnic minority groups, especially black people, and have high rates of membership and attendance **e**.

ⓔ This is another strong paragraph. **c** Two important and relevant concepts are introduced and explained, with the authors correctly identified. **d** The student then explains why these concepts could be used to explain the churchgoing habits of some members of ethnic minority groups. **e** A good example is given of a particular kind of church with a strong ethnic minority membership. Note that the student has picked up the reference in the Item to 'black people'.

> Another reason could be the fact that going to a weekly act of worship helps people from ethnic minority groups establish a sense of community with others from a similar background **f**. Many churches with high proportions of members from these groups offer a wide range of other facilities, not just the chance to worship together. It is quite common for such churches to have playgroups, sports teams, old people's clubs etc. and to offer a variety of kinds of support to members. Especially for recent immigrants, such things would be very important in helping to establish a sense of belonging **g**.

ⓔ The student here **f** offers another suitable reason and **g** gives a clear example. Note how there is a strong focus on the set question — this is especially important in these shorter answers.

> Finally, many ethnic minority people come from societies that are much less secular than Britain **h**. This means that they have a cultural tradition of churchgoing that has been lost in many Western societies which have undergone the process of secularisation **i**.

ⓔ **h** The student concludes with another good reason, which is clearly explained, and **i** uses another appropriate sociological concept.

ⓔ **AO1: 6/6 + AO2: 12/12 = 18/18 marks**

> **(03)** The term 'fundamentalism' is frequently used in a narrow way to describe primarily Islamist groups, often extremist in their views, such as those that came to prominence after the invasion of Iraq by Western coalition groups in 2003, and it is these groups that have caused concern to (Western) society and led to conflict **a**, i.e. the 'war on terror'. However, a more sociological definition refers to any religious group that challenges modernity and tries to bring its followers back to what it believes are the 'fundamental' beliefs expressed in its holy writings **b**. So, although the term fundamentalist is increasingly associated with Islam, it is important to note that there are fundamentalist groups in many major religions, including Christianity, Hinduism, Buddhism and Judaism **c**.

ⓔ This is a very strong opening paragraph displaying good knowledge and understanding, as well as analysis and evaluation. **a** After describing how the term is often used, and referring this back to the question, **b** a more sociological definition of the concept is given, followed by **c** examples of other religions that contain fundamentalist groups.

> Kepel looked at the rise of Islamic fundamentalism which led to the overthrow of the Shah of Iran in 1978. Iran had been one of the more liberal and 'Westernised'

Arab countries, but after growing dissatisfaction with the Shah's rule, the cleric Ayatollah Khomenei came back from exile and established an Islamist state based on Islamic law. Kepel said that the message from the religious leaders was that modernism had failed, the reason being that the people had moved away from the 'fundamentals' of Islam **d**. The attention of the West was again focused on Islamic fundamentalism following the 9/11 attacks in the USA, which were quickly attributed to Osama bin Laden and the Al Qaeda group. The notion of suicide bombers who were prepared to sacrifice themselves for their faith further strengthened the stereotypical view of Islamic fundamentalism and led to the 'war on terror' against such groups. The stereotype was further strengthened by the London bombings of 2005 **e**.

🅔 **d** While accurate, the discussion of Kepel and the Iranian revolution is not clearly linked to the question, although it could have been. **e** However, the examples included give evidence regarding why Islamist fundamentalist groups were considered of concern to the West and linked to social conflict in the form of terrorism.

If we look at some of the fundamentalist groups in the Christian faith, we can also see that they can easily come into conflict with liberal groups in society. In the USA, members of Christian fundamentalist groups (often referred to as the New Christian Right) are opposed, sometimes violently, to abortion, gay marriage/civil partnerships, homosexuality in general and what some would see as the more liberal expression of ideas in the arts and the media, e.g. 'Jerry Springer: the Opera'. The influence of these groups extends into politics, with some possible contenders for the US presidency coming from this background. It is possible that a future president of the USA could be a Christian fundamentalist, something that would be of concern to many people both in and outside the USA **f**. In education, the belief of some Christian fundamentalists in creationism or 'intelligent design' has brought them into conflict with more mainstream views of science. Bruce points out that fundamentalist groups in the USA have become very good at using new technologies to spread their message, producing very slick television programmes spreading their message (televangelism) and creating what are in effect huge stage shows in churches seating several thousand people on Sundays. This helps to spread their message and can give them a strong political voice **g**.

🅔 **f** Here is an example from Christianity, with a clear explanation of some causes of conflict, **g** followed by an example of one way in which the message of fundamentalism is spread and a possible consequence.

An important question for sociologists is why there should be a rise in fundamentalist groups in different religions **h**. Davie believes that people are increasingly concerned over what are seen as the failures of modernism to deliver a 'good' society, so that people look to a more 'religious' past to try to recover what are seen as better ways of managing society and the environment.

She points out that what are seen as the 'essential truths' tend to relate to the pressures of modern global economies. Bauman argues that fundamentalism is seen as providing certainties in an uncertain world, and gives followers an unchallengeable moral code by which to live their lives. Others have argued that the 'war on terror' against Islamist fundamentalist groups has only served to recruit even more people to their cause, particularly young men, who see the USA as 'the great Satan', and the West as morally bankrupt **i**.

(e) **h** In this paragraph the student picks up on the important point in the question about the 'rise' in fundamentalist groups, **i**.and offers some explanations from different sociologists.

In conclusion, while there does seem to be an increase in the membership of fundamentalist groups in several different religions, the 'cause for concern' depends on which groups are being looked at, who is likely to be affected, and in what way. So while for some there may be 'cause for concern', for others the rise of fundamentalism would be seen as a good thing, especially as a counter-measure to modernism and secularisation.

(e) This is a strong conclusion. It 'unpicks' the question and is clearly based on the arguments and evidence presented in the answer.

(e) **AO1: 12/15 + AO2 (a): 7/9 + AO2 (b): 8/9 = 27/33 marks**

(e) **Overall: 51/60 marks**

C-grade student

(01) • Older people are nearer to death, so are more likely to want to go to church to be sure of being in a 'state of grace' when they die so they can go to heaven.

• Older people are more used to going to church, as it was the done thing when they were younger.

• Older people are often lonely.

(e) The first two reasons are acceptable, and each has a suitable explanation, although the second point might have included the concept of 'socialisation' to make it more sociological. The third point might have scored some marks if it had been explained in such a way that it was clearly linked to the question. As it is, there is insufficient information to gain any marks.

(e) **6/9 marks**

(02) Item A shows that secularisation is not happening as much as some sociologists claim **a**. It points out that many churches are in a healthier state now than they were 7 years ago. However, only 6.3% of people are in church on a Sunday, and there is a high percentage of older churchgoers, which could make things worse in the future.

ⓔ This answer has not got off to a good start. **a** Although the student refers to Item A, the reference to the question is not at all clear, and it looks as though the answer is in danger of becoming about secularisation, which is not what the question is about. It is a good idea to refer to the Item, but make sure that you choose the part that is relevant to the question. Apart from the last few words of the paragraph, material from the Item is simply repeated, rather than interpreted and/or analysed.

> Item A also says that a number of churches are growing, and that there is a considerable increase in the number of ethnic minority churchgoers, especially black people **b**. Some churches are growing because they are offering the kind of service that some people want, such as the Alpha course, which can get thousands of people to join up **c**. Other churches, especially the Catholic ones, are growing because they get lots of people from Eastern Europe, such as Poles **d**, who tend to be much more religious than British people.

ⓔ Bearing in mind that this is an 18-mark question, and should take only about 20 minutes, this student is in danger of losing marks by simply not addressing the set question. **b** Although a relevant part is picked out of the Item, the point is not followed up, and **c** the example refers to the growth in churches, rather than focusing on ethnic minority churchgoers. **d** The final point could be made relevant to the question, as Polish migrants are an ethnic minority group, but the relevance to the question is left implicit.

> We are left with the question of why ethnic minority people, especially black people, should be more likely to go to church **d**. There a number of possible reasons for this. A lot of black people go to Pentecostal or evangelical churches, whose services are usually quite different to those of the mainstream English churches. There is a lot of singing and clapping, and sometimes members of the congregation 'speak in tongues' **e**.

ⓔ **d** At last, the student begins to address the set question. **e** However, the rest of the paragraph does not really follow this up, instead it gives an example of the kind of church likely to be attended by black worshippers. This should now be linked to the reasons, or this answer will not have answered the question.

> From the start of mass immigration from the Caribbean in the 1950s through to newer arrivals from different parts of Africa, black people have been more likely to be churchgoers than native British people. One main reason is that Christianity is very strong in these countries, and the practice of group worship, rather than praying at home, is very strong **f**. Even for fourth and fifth generation immigrants, the culture has been passed down. So going to church to worship is rooted in their culture **g**. Many churches with large black congregations are found in inner city areas, where many black people live. More than two-thirds of Sunday churchgoers in London are black. The Glory House church in East London regularly gets about 2,000 people to its services. Churches with mainly black congregations are known as BMCs — Black Majority Churches. **h**

AQA A2 Sociology

(e) The student finally begins to focus on the question, **f** giving a reason and **g** applying this to longer-standing migrants. **h** Knowledge and understanding is shown by the reference to BMCs.

> BMCs are often 24/7 churches — that is to say that their doors are always open, and they provide a range of services and facilities for their congregations, something which would be very helpful especially to more recent immigrants **i**. They often have a strong outreach programme with many links to the community, and can also work with social services, youth workers and the police, e.g. to reduce gang warfare **j**. This work is often carried out by people called 'street pastors'. BMCs are also often quite wealthy, as many evangelicals and Pentecostalists regularly give money to their church in the form of tithes **k**. So, rather than something that is just open on a Sunday, these churches are completely integrated into the lives of their congregation, which would help to explain why they continue to worship **l**.

(e) **i** Another reason for the churchgoing habits of black migrants is given and **j** the example of the importance of the outreach programmes is useful. **k** It is not made clear how the reference to the wealth of the churches is relevant, though implicitly one could see that the revenue would be helpful in providing the kinds of service mentioned. **l** The final sentence attempts to draw the preceding material together, but is rather weak.

> Of course, ethnic minority people doesn't only mean people from the Caribbean and Africa. As well as the Eastern Europeans, there is a large Asian population in Britain, many of them being very religious **m**. Although the Item is about 'churches', i.e. Christianity, worship at other places such as mosques and temples is also strong. The reasons are partly the same as for black people, but some ethnic minority groups, e.g. Muslims, have some practices that can bring them into conflict with some of the values of mainstream society (e.g. attitudes to women) so belonging to their local congregation can help to strengthen their sense of community **n**. Many mosques also offer religious teaching to younger people, which would also be a reason for people to attend **n**.

(e) It is a pity that material such as this was not used earlier, where it could have been developed. Here, however, **m** the student recognises different ethnic minority groups and their religiosity, and **n** ends with two appropriate reasons why Muslims might be religious observers.

(e) **AO1: 4/6 + AO2: 7/12 = 11/18 marks**

> **(03)** Sociologists like Durkheim believed that one of the main functions of religion was to achieve consensus in society. In this view, religion is the 'moral glue' that helps to bind a society together **a**. Marx thought that religion was part of the ideological state apparatus **b** and could help prevent conflict (proletarian revolution) by being the 'opium of the people' and helping to deaden their pain so they did not realise that they were being exploited by the bourgeoisie and try to overthrow them **a**. Critics of Durkheim point out that he based his ideas on simple societies and that they did not apply to large industrial societies **b**.

e **a** This is a reasonably good introduction. It offers the views of two sociologists to illustrate the opinion that religion can be thought of as achieving consensus in society, rather than conflict, as suggested by the question. **b** Note the relevant use of a sociological concept — always try to use appropriate sociological language where possible.

> However, nowadays religion is often associated with conflict, such as in Northern Ireland, Iraq and Afghanistan. Even as far back as the Crusades religion was associated with war and conflict. So the view expressed in the question is nothing new **c**.

e While the examples offered are correct, they are not made relevant to the question, which is specifically about religious fundamentalism. **c** The student has not (at least yet) shown that he/she understands the particular focus of the question.

> Religious fundamentalists are people who often have extreme views about their religion and are often prepared to fight and often die for their beliefs **d**. An example of this would be Islamic fundamentalists, such as the suicide bombers in London in July 2005 and the people who flew the planes into the twin towers in the USA on 9/11 **e**. There have been other examples of suicide bombers in many different countries, most of them religious fanatics. So what are fundamentalists? They are people who believe utterly in a holy book or similar which they think tells them how their life should be led **f**. While their societies are stable, there is not usually a problem, but when a society starts to modernise and new ideas are introduced, then the fundamentalists are usually critical, and say that society is moving away from the basic beliefs, which is wrong **g**.

e Here the student at last begins to focus on the set question, **d** offering a description of fundamentalists together with **e** some examples of those thought to have martyred themselves for their beliefs. There is then **f** a brief definition with **g** a comment on why fundamentalist groups might emerge.

> In some cases, such as with Ayatollah Khomeini in Iran and the Taliban in Afghanistan, fundamentalists come to hold political as well as religious power, which can give them a great hold over society. Some writers believe that so-called terrorist movements such as Al Qaeda are in fact more about politics than religion **h**. Research by Sageman about 172 people in the Al Qaeda network showed that most of them had not, in fact, had a strong religious upbringing at all, and one of the London bombers was only a recent convert to Islam **i**.

e This is potentially a very important paragraph, in which the student tries **h** to explore the links between religion and politics with regard to fundamentalist groups, and **i** provides an interesting example from research. However, the relevance to the set question remains largely implicit, and as yet the student has not picked up on whether conflict is 'inevitable'.

> There have been other examples of fundamentalism and conflict, not military or violent conflict but social conflict **j**. There was a huge outcry from Muslims when a Danish newspaper published what were seen as disrespectful cartoons of the prophet Mohammed **k**, and in France it is now illegal for women to wear the full burka in public, and some women have been arrested for doing this **k**. Some other countries are also thinking of bringing in the ban, which is likely to cause more conflict.

(e) **j** An interesting distinction is made here between military/violent conflict and social conflict, with **k** two examples offered. This aspect might have been usefully pursued. However, the student has lost the focus on fundamentalist groups, and has broadened the discussion to speak of 'Muslims', which is quite different.

> It is not clear whether religious fundamentalist groups will continue to grow. A lot depends on the West and whether it continues to intervene in Arab and Muslim countries, as it seems that this raises such hostility on the part of deeply religious people that their response can easily be one of conflict **l**. So we may see more religious conflict in the future.

(e) **l** Again, a potentially important point is raised but is not really followed through. Overall, the student shows reasonably good knowledge and understanding, but there is not always a clear focus on the set question. One weakness of this answer is the exclusive focus on Islamic fundamentalist groups to the neglect of those in other faiths, and there is no discussion of whether fundamentalism necessarily leads to conflict. However, though narrow in focus, the answer is broadly sociological.

(e) **AO1: 10/15 + AO2 (a): 6/9 + AO2 (b): 4/9 = 20/33 marks**

(e) **Overall: 37/60 marks**

Example 4 Religion on the web; religiosity; New Religious Movements

Read Item A below and answer questions 01 and 02 that follow. Then answer question 03.

Item A

Virtually all religious groups now have a presence on the web. This means not only the major religions and denominations, but also groups representing forms of Wicca, paganism and various forms of 'New Age' spirituality. Helland (2004) says that, by its very structure, the internet has an affinity with patterns of religious participation in late-modern Western societies. First, it allows those who are highly motivated with regard to religious matters to channel their religiosity without the need to commit to any particular official religious organisation or institution. Second, it allows people to log on when they feel the need. As an example of this, Helland uses the example of the events of 9/11 in the USA. Following the attacks, hundreds of thousands of people began to post online prayers, light online candles and enter into religiously-based web dialogue. Many religious websites began to devote whole sections to Islam, creating avenues for people to learn more about Islamic traditions.

Source: adapted from J. Garrod (2009) 'Religion in cyberspace', *Sociology Review*, Vol. 19 No. 2.

(01) Identify and briefly explain three advantages, other than those mentioned in Item A, to religious groups of having a presence on the internet. (9 marks)

ⓔ Make sure that you give only advantages, and avoid any mentioned in the Item.

(02) Using material from Item A and elsewhere, examine how web-based religious sites might make it more difficult to measure the extent of religiosity in society. (18 marks)

ⓔ Think about the concept of 'religiosity' — is there a consensus on how this is defined? Make sure that you use relevant material from the Item, and keep your answer focused on web-based religious sites, rather than measuring religiosity in general. You may not have come across much material on this aspect of the topic in your textbooks, so this question really asks you to apply your sociological imagination.

(03) Assess the view that the increase in New Religious Movements is largely a response to deprivation. (33 marks)

ⓔ There are three important aspects to consider in this question. What are New Religious Movements? What evidence is there for an increase in them? If the evidence suggests that there is, to what extent might this be a response to deprivation?

Total: 60 marks

A-grade student

(01) ● A presence on the web allows religious groups to be accessed by people who might not otherwise have heard about them, thus increasing the potential to recruit new members.

● It is cheaper to put information on the web than to print lots of leaflets and booklets. This would be important for smaller religious groups who might not have much money.

● By using video clips, groups could make their sermons available to anyone, not just those who could attend the place of worship.

ⓔ Three acceptable reasons, each clearly explained.

ⓔ **9/9 marks**

(02) An important thing to consider here is what we mean by 'religiosity', which will affect how we measure it **a**. If we mean religious thoughts or beliefs, then usually the only way to measure this is to undertake some kind of survey. This has problems, e.g. with achieving a representative sample, and then knowing whether people are actually telling the truth **b**. If we mean practising religion in some way, then the usual way is to find out how many people attend places of worship and how often, and this is very difficult to know with accuracy. It is also difficult to say for sure that people who attend places of worship are always 'religious' — for some, it is a social thing **b**.

ⓔ **a** The student has immediately recognised that there are problems associated with the concept of 'religiosity'. **b** Two problems with measuring the extent of religiosity are then raised, with examples.

So, given that there are problems with measuring religiosity anyway, how could religious websites make this even more difficult? If we wanted to do a survey, then a question about visiting religious websites could be included, so that wouldn't make things any more difficult. However, people might not be visiting particular sites for what we might call 'religious' reasons — they might simply be curious **c**. Item A points out that after 9/11 some sites started to devote sections to Islam **d**, so people might visit the site for reasons of curiosity rather than because of religious feelings. If we look at actually measuring religiosity, then websites do make this more difficult **e**. Sociologists could ask the religious groups who have sites to let them know how many 'hits' they receive. However, first they may not wish to answer, second they may lie and exaggerate the number, and third, even if they told the truth, no one would know the reason that people were visiting the site in the first place. It might just be curiosity. Of course, there is the problem with measuring attendance at places of worship that people might also not go for proper religious reasons, as already mentioned. However, it is more likely that if they make the effort to go to a church, mosque etc. they are in some way more likely to be religious than people who can just get on to a religious website with the click of a mouse. People are unlikely physically to visit several different kinds of places of worship, but it is much easier when many sites can be visited when sitting at home at the computer **f**.

e Here there is a strong focus on the set question. **c** The student looks again at how religiosity might be measured, but this time applies it to religious sites, also showing evaluation. **d** There is an appropriate reference to Item A, **e, f** followed by another discussion closely linked to the question, again showing analysis and evaluation.

> Finally, Item A points out that religious websites allow people to explore religious ideas and issues without committing to any particular group or organisation **g**. Davie refers to this as 'believing without belonging' **h**. Given that, as Item A says, almost all 'religious' groups now have a website, including things like New Age beliefs **g**, then it seems as though such sites would indeed make it more difficult to measure the extent of religiosity in society **i**.

e **g** Two more appropriate references to the Item — note how the student does not simply repeat the words, but interprets them. **h** An important sociological concept is introduced and **i** the student finishes by drawing a conclusion about the relationship between religious websites and measuring religiosity.

e **AO1: 5/6 + AO2: 12/12 = 17/18 marks**

> **(03)** The idea that some poor and/or marginalised people will turn to certain religious groups for comfort and understanding to help them bear their position in society comes from Weber, who referred to it as the 'theodicy of disprivilege' **a**. Some have suggested that the growth in New Religious Movements in recent times has been because more and more people are in this position and are turning to NRMs because they feel that established religions have let them down or do not provide the answers they are looking for **b**.

e The student makes a good start with a strong focus on the set question. **a** Weber's concept is appropriately used, and **b** successfully interpreted to link it to the issue raised by the question.

> Before going any further, we should ask what New Religious Movements actually are. There is no single agreed definition, but most people use the term to refer to groups outside the main established faiths which have emerged, especially in Western Europe and the USA, since the end of the Second World War, and particularly since the 1960s **c**. Obviously this covers a huge number of groups, so Wallis made an attempt to classify them into three main groups. These were (i) world affirming, (ii) world rejecting and (iii) world accommodating **d**. It is important to remember that these are ideal types, and it will not always be easy to fit a particular group into a category. Briefly, world-affirming groups are those aimed at releasing members' 'inner potential' to help them succeed in today's world. Examples are Scientology, Transcendental Meditation (TM) and Erhard Seminars Training. Many also put so-called 'New Age' movements in this category. **e** World-rejecting groups are those that ask members to withdraw from the world, which is seen as flawed and corrupt. They demand huge commitment from members, and many are millenarian (expecting some cosmic event that will cleanse the world of evil). Examples are the Moonies, the People's Temple and Heaven's Gate. Some of these groups have become notorious through their

links to the mass suicide of members or even terrorist attacks, e.g. Aum Supreme Truth in Japan **e**. World-accommodating groups are those that are either content with the world, or indifferent to it, choosing to focus instead on the 'inner spiritual life' of members, usually through prayer and collective worship. An example would be the neo-Pentecostals, who try to achieve a 'charismatic renewal' of the spiritual life of Christians **e**.

(e) **c** This is another strong paragraph which tries to identify what NRMs are. **d** Wallis' typology is used correctly, and **e** a brief explanation and example is given for each group.

When we come to try to see what kind of people become members of these groups, we hit a major problem. While some groups are quite 'open' (e.g. Scientology), others, especially world-rejecting groups, are more 'closed' and secretive, and it is difficult to find any kind of accurate information about the social background of members **f**. There is an additional problem that many NRMs are very short-lived, so by the time that a sociologist might wish to do research on them, they have already disbanded. However, we do have some information that can help to answer the question about a link between membership of NRMs and deprivation **f**.

(e) There is still a strong focus on the question. The student shows both knowledge and evaluation by raising **f** two problems of identifying who joins NRMs. Note that the temptation to give lots of detail about certain NRMs has been avoided — it is always important to make sure that the material used is relevant to the question set.

Bruce suggests that membership of world-affirming groups is largely white and middle-class, with more women than men belonging to such groups **g**. Partly this is because these groups don't ask for any kind of break with a conventional lifestyle, and don't place awkward restrictions on people's behaviour. They have a particular appeal to people who might already be fairly successful in life, but want to become even more so. The groups themselves tend to be very successful, using slick marketing techniques to spread their message **h**. Among the many 'New Age' movements, members also tend to be largely middle-class. (Bruce says that this is because genuinely poor people don't have the time to worry about their 'inner self' — they are more concerned with putting food on the table.) Membership of world-affirming groups would not then be linked to deprivation **i**.

(e) **g** The views of a sociologist are successfully applied to the question. **h** Reasons are given for the view and **i** there is a strong link back to the question.

Wallis thought that world-rejecting groups would be those most likely to appeal to poor and marginalised people, with their emphasis on withdrawing from the world and becoming part of a supportive 'family' **j**. However, Lantenari argues that members tend to be white, middle class and educated, and says that these are not the 'religions of the oppressed'. Barker's study of the Moonies also found that members tended to come from secure middle-class homes. Such groups also have a very high dropout rate, suggesting that people only 'withdraw' from the world temporarily **k**. It is also important to note that world-rejecting NRMs usually have only a very small membership **l**.

e **j** A second group is examined, and again there is a strong link to the set question. **k** Evaluation is shown by reference to Barker's work and **l** a comment on the size of membership.

Not much is said about world-accommodating groups, but Aldridge says that these too have a mainly middle-class membership. Also, they tend to exist within the realm of established Christian (Pentecostal) churches, rather than as completely separate groups **m**.

Finally, we should look at what is happening to NRMs. It is claimed that overall membership is in decline, with the important exception of world-affirming groups, who seem to be growing in popularity **n**. This could be linked to the self-centredness of the so-called 'me' generation. In any case, these are the groups with a predominantly middle-class membership and appeal, so it would be hard to argue that overall the growth in NRMs is linked to deprivation **o**.

e **m** There is a brief mention of the third type of NRM, justified by the accurate claim that little is written about them. **n** The final paragraph is strong: there is a comment about the differential growth of NRMs and another strong link back to the set question. **o** The conclusion is justified by the arguments and evidence put forward in the rest of the answer. Note that this is a particularly strong answer, and many students would not be able to achieve this level. However, it could be used as guidance regarding how a really good answer can be constructed.

e **AO1: 15/15 + AO2 (a): 9/9 + AO2(b): 9/9 = 33/33 marks**

e **Overall: 59/60 marks**

(01) • It is easier for people to find out about religious groups who might not have a base near where they live, allowing groups to reach more people.

• It would be possible for people who could not get out of their home, e.g. disabled, to listen to web-based sermons and have discussions with other people. Religious groups could then find new members who wouldn't have been able to come to their services.

• Religious groups could be available with a presence 24/7, so people could log on whenever they wanted or needed to.

e The first two reasons and their explanations are acceptable, so gain two points each. The third, point, however, is one that is given in the Item, so does not count. It is important to read the instructions given in the question very carefully, to avoid losing marks.

e **6/9 marks**

(02) Religiosity means whether people believe and practise religion **a**. Sociologists have been interested to measure the amount of religiosity there is in society to see whether it is shrinking. This helps them to see whether secularisation is increasing in a society **b**. Sociologists do not agree about whether secularisation is happening or not, and if it is, to what extent. There is a debate about whether things such as New Age beliefs and practices should be counted as religious or not **c**. This is where knowing the amount of religiosity becomes very important.

ⓔ **a** The definition of religiosity is not quite accurate, but the student realises that its meaning is important to the question. **b** The concept is then linked appropriately to secularisation, **c** but then the thrust of the question is lost, and the answer is sidetracked into a discussion about secularisation. Especially in these shorter-answer questions, it is important not to lose focus on the set question. Even if accurate, material that is not relevant to the question will not score marks.

Surveys have shown that overall church attendance is falling, even though some churches are doing well, especially those that have congregations from the ethnic minority community. Sociologists though don't agree that this necessarily means that people are less religious, as this is only looking at whether they go to church or not. The 2001 Census asked a question about religious belief for the first time, and 92% of people answered the question, although it was voluntary. Of those, just over three-quarters reported that they had a religion, suggesting that there is a high degree of religiosity in society **d**.

ⓔ **d** Again, while the material here is accurate, the focus seems to be on church attendance, religious belief and secularisation, rather than on how religious websites might make measuring religiosity more difficult.

If three-quarters of people say they have a religion, but only a fraction of them go to church, then looking at church membership and attendance is not a very accurate way of measuring religiosity. Religious internet sites could make this even more difficult **e**. First it would be very hard to find out how many people were visiting these sites, although some sites have a kind of 'counter' at the bottom showing how many hits there have been. This is not always helpful, as some people could visit the site several times, and get counted each time. It also wouldn't tell us why they visited the site — were they taking part in some kind of religious blog to share ideas, were they curious to find something out about that particular group, or were they having some kind of religious experience (e.g. by reading sacred texts or the words of as particular preacher) **f**? As Item A says, they could be online to post prayers, as they did after 9/11 **g**. We should remember too that not everybody has a computer, so there would be lots of people who were unable to look at religious sites even if they wanted to **h**.

ⓔ **e** At last, the student begins to address the question. **f** Some relevant information is provided showing how religious sites might make the measurement of religiosity even more difficult than before. **g** There is also a belated reference to the Item. **h** The final comment is potentially an important one, but is not developed or made relevant to the question.

In conclusion, religious sites can fill a number of different functions for people, so they could make the measurement of religiosity more difficult.

ⓔ This is a fairly weak conclusion that adds little, but does at least attempt to provide an answer to the set question.

ⓔ **AO1: 3/6 + AO2: 7/12 = 10/18 marks**

(03) New Religious Movements sprang up after the Second World War. They were 'new' because they did not belong to any of the established world religions, although some of them borrowed ideas from Eastern religions such as Buddhism. Many sociologists prefer to use the term NRM rather than 'cult', because the word cult has come to be applied to more sinister groups **a**.

ⓔ **a** This is a good beginning that explains clearly what is generally meant by NRMs, together with a reason why the term is used.

Wallis classified NRMs into three groups — world affirming, world rejecting and world accommodating **b**. World-affirming groups such as Scientology promise members that they will be shown how to release their inner potential and become more successful in life. World-rejecting groups want to shut themselves off from the world and live a particular kind of lifestyle. This kind of group often seems to attract people that we might think of as fanatics, as they are sometimes prepared to die for their beliefs. Examples are the People's Temple at Jonestown, Guyana, where almost 1,000 people committed suicide at the order of their leader, Jim Jones. Another example is the US UFO Heaven's Gate group, where 39 members committed suicide in order to reach (as they believed) an alien space craft that was following the Hale Bopp comet **c**. Examples of larger world rejecting groups are the Moonies and Hare Krishna. World-accommodating groups accept the world as it is.

ⓔ **b** Here is a relevant and accurate mention of Wallis' classification, together with some examples. **c** However, there was no need to go into detail about the world-rejecting groups.

Weber thought that some sects would attract poor and deprived people because they explained their poverty and low social position as God's will and a way of testing their faith. This could be the link between some NRMs and deprivation **d**. Wallis thought that some world-rejecting sects would appeal to people who had been marginalised **d**. You can see how this could work, if people who felt rejected by society wanted to turn away from it and find comfort with a group that told them that they were, in fact, the 'chosen ones' **e**. It is not easy, though, to find out exactly who joins these groups, as some of them are very secretive and suspicious of any attempt to find out more about them **f**. In fact, the Jonestown suicides took place because a Congressman had organised a visit to Jonestown to see what was going on, as there were reports of beatings and torture of members, especially those who said that they wanted to leave. As well as the suicides, the Congressman was killed as he was about to leave to go back to the USA.

(e) **d** There is a good reference to two sociologists who suggested a link between certain NRMs and deprivation, **e** together with a brief analysis of why there might be such a link. **f** The student then gives a difficulty of finding out about such group members. The Jonestown example, though relevant to the point made, is unnecessarily detailed.

> Barker and Bruce both say that members of some NRMs are largely middle class and not deprived. Barker found this out when she did research on the Moonies, and Bruce found the same when he looked at some New Age groups. Woodhead and Heelas found the same when they looked at New Age practices in the Kendal Project **g**.

(e) **g** The student gives three examples of sociologists who have found no evidence of the social deprivation of members in certain NRMs. However, it is not made clear that the groups looked at by Bruce and Heelas were not world-rejecting groups, but world-affirming ones.

> So we can see that while in theory NRMs might appeal to deprived people, in practice this has not been proved. Still, some groups come and go very quickly and some are hard to access, so we can't be absolutely sure about this **h**.

(e) **h** This is a very brief conclusion, though there is an attempt to answer the set question.

(e) **AO1: 10/15 + AO2 (a): 6/9 + AO2 (b): 4/9 = 20/33 marks**

(e) **Overall: 36/60 marks**

Knowledge check answers

1 The worldwide fan base of Manchester United football club and the devoted and fanatical way that supporters follow the fortunes of the team can be seen as a quasi-religion.

2 The Qu'ran and the Bible are sacred objects in Islam and Christianity respectively.

3 A system of production is the way that a society organises how it produces the goods and services that are necessary for social life.

4 Alienation is the objective condition where the producers of goods and services have no stake in the production process or the products of their labour.

5 Possible answers include: all parts of society contribute to the maintenance of the whole; society is essentially harmonious; society is composed of the interrelationships between its constituent parts; it is a structuralist theory.

6 Existential refers to the conditions of our existence, in contrast to more spiritual or supernatural concerns.

7 Possible answers include: the decrease in importance of national societies; the growth of international organisations' power; technological links worldwide that make for 'instant news'.

8 Identification through difference, where individuals identify with each other because they need the services and goods that each differentially provides.

9 The Church of England or the Anglican Church.

10 Legitimising is where beliefs or events function to create consent in subordinate groups to the control of society by those in superordinate positions.

11 Possible answers include: action in an organisation to produce a profit; ploughing back profits into a business; seeking to minimise risks to an enterprise.

12 Objective reality refers to situations and structures that seem to exist independently of the individuals who inhabit them and therefore have an existence beyond those individuals.

13 The most commonly cited cult is the Church of Scientology.

14 An example of the Roman Catholic Church being conservative is in its attitude to homosexuality and being radical is liberation theology.

15 The Tea Party movement.

16 Possible answers include: Methodists, Primitive Methodists, Salvation Army, Presbyterian Church.

17 Theology is the system of beliefs associated with a particular religion, encompassing aspects such as the nature of God, the problem of evil, the correct ways to worship etc.

18 Hybrid identities.

19 Modernity is characterised by the scientific frame of mind, the rational approach to social issues and an attitude of certainty towards scientific knowledge.

20 Born into us.

21 Possible answers include: healthcare, education, politics.

22 That some secular ideas can stand in the place of religion and fulfil the functions that were previously carried out by religious ideas.

23 Max Weber.

24 That a view is biased towards a particular ethnic point of view (usually white and Western).

Page numbers in **bold** refer to **key term definitions**

A

age and religion 43–52, 61–69
'à la carte' religion 14
alienation 11
anti-secularisation 37–38
anti-social behaviour 36
apartheid **20**
atrophy 33

B

baptism 21, 22
believing without belonging 36
body **29**
bourgeoisie **11**–12
bureaucratisation **33**

C

Calvinism 10, 11, 19
capitalism 10, 11, 12, 19
catharsis 26
Catholic Church 10, 11, 19, 33
change, religion as source of 19–20, 53–60
charisma **25**, 32
choice overload 14–15
Christianity 16, 21, 28, 33, 36
church attendance 33, 34, 35, 43–52, 61–69
churches 21–22, 23
class and religion 26–27
client cults 25
cognitive reductionism 14
collective rituals **9**, 12
compensators 27
conflict, religion as source of 17–18, 61–69
conscience collective 9
conservative force of religion 18–19, 53–60
crime 36
cross-culturalism 11
cults 22–23, 27

D

de-Christianisation 33
definitions of religion 8–9, 53–60
denominations 22–23, 27
diasporic populations **16**
disenchantment 35

Disneyfication 15
divine right of kings **21**
dominant social class **26**
Durkheim, Émile 9–10, 12

E

ecclesiae 24
economic conflicts **17**
ecumenicalism 18, 33
elective affinity 10
essentialism 8
ethnic identity and religion 29–30, 61–69
exceptionalism 35
exclusivist definitions 8, 9, **32**

F

false consciousness 11, 14
formalism 22
functionalism 8, 9, 12–13
fundamentalism 15, 30–31, 61–69

G

gender and religion 28–29
globalisation 15
global society 16

H

Hinduism 27
House Church movement **35**

I

identity 29–30
ideology **8**, 11, 16
inclusivist definitions 8, **32**
inspirationalism **22**
interactionism 13–14
interest theorists 26
internet 15, 70–77
Islam 16, 18, 28, 31

J

Judaism 16, 28

L

Lebenswelt **13**
liberation theology 20
libido **28**

M

Marx, Karl 11–12
Marxism 12, 17, 26, 34